This book of Christmas cheer belongs to:

_____

_____

A
VERY PRAIRIE
Christmas
BAKEBOOK

COOKIES, CANDIES, CAKES & MORE:
VINTAGE BAKING TO
CELEBRATE THE FESTIVE SEASON

KARLYNN JOHNSTON

aka The Kitchen Magpie

appetite
by RANDOM HOUSE

*For all of my readers who keep the spirit
of Christmas in their hearts 365 days a year,
this book's for you. Merry Christmas from
my family to yours!*

Appetite by Random House® and colophon are registered trademarks
of Penguin Random House LLC.

Library and Archives of Canada Cataloguing in Publication is available
upon request.
ISBN: 978-0-525-61148-6
eBook ISBN: 978-0-525-61149-3

Photography by Karlynn Johnston. Additional photography on pages
3, 6, 8, 11, 12, 39, 248, 251, 255, and 275 by Luminarie Creative
Cover and book design by Kate Sinclair
Printed in China

Published in Canada by Appetite by Random House®, a division of
Penguin Random House Canada Limited

www.penguinrandomhouse.ca

10 9 8 7 6 5 4 3 2 1

CONTENTS

CHRISTMAS ON THE PRAIRIES

This, my friends, is the cookbook I have been dreaming about writing for years.

I am unabashedly THAT person when it comes to Christmas. I start humming Christmas tunes in October while my Halloween decorations are up. I put up three Christmas trees every year: a 1960s silver aluminum tree, a 1960s green aluminum tree, and one faux fir tree (which my kids insist on), all of which go up, without fail, the day after Remembrance Day. (Let me confess, I own still another three vintage trees that don't always get decorated, simply because I run out of room.) And as soon as I pack away the Christmas turkey leftovers, I am already dreaming about how I will decorate the house next year and what we will cook up.

I've always wondered if my love of the holiday season stems from our notoriously, bone-chillingly cold winters on the Canadian Prairies, with copious amounts of snowfall that astonish people who don't live here and seemingly never end for those of us who do. If we are lucky, the snow holds off until the kids have enjoyed Halloween, but when I was a kid, trick-or-treating involved costumes pulled over my snowsuit! Christmas becomes a wonderful bright spot in our long winter and, if you're like me, can be stretched out for a solid two months of decorations, lights, and entertainment. Ukrainian Christmas celebrations don't begin until January 6 (more on that on page 17), so we wait until after that to take everything down.

During our cold Prairie winters, our pace of life slows down, whether we want it to or not. Our attention shifts from the outdoors to the indoors. Outside activities lessen, as even the most diehard skaters, skiers, and snowshoers stay inside when the mercury dips below –30°C. Occasionally, we get snow days from work and school. Outings at the lake turn into board games around the table. Mowing the lawn turns into shoveling the sidewalks and hurrying back inside as soon as you can.

But it can be lovely. With that change of pace can come more time to bake and cook. And the food—oh, the food that we have only during the holiday season! The glorious, once-a-year baking fest where we pull out all the stops.

From the middle of November onward, I take great joy in planning, baking, and freezing goodies for Christmas. Even though it's the busiest time of year for my website (my website traffic quadruples during the holidays, with everyone wanting recipes), I truly live for every moment of holiday baking as soon as those first few flakes of snow fall until Ukrainian Christmas on January 7. (Then I am so done with all the baking and cooking, and survive simply on soup until spring.)

You will see some recipes here that also appeared in one of my first two books, *Flapper Pie and a Blue Prairie Sky* and *The Prairie Table*. There are some treats, like my quintessential Traditional Whipped Shortbread (page 28) and my Thin & Chewy Snickerdoodles (page 41), that simply could NOT be left out of a baking book that is all about Christmas on the Prairies. So if you have my other books, first of all, thank you! Second, forgive the repeat recipes, but rest assured that it's recipes like these, which reflect baking on the Prairies perfectly, that make this the perfect cookbook to gift to loved ones and pass down to your kids. Plus, there's over 120 recipes in this book, giving you so many new ones to enjoy! (In fact, I have so many cookie recipes, they fill two chapters!)

Mr. Kitchen Magpie (aka my husband, Mike) once again gets the closing chapter, full of punches and libations. He took on the task of creating a safe eggnog (page 261) that cooks the egg yolk and can be enjoyed by everyone—which can, of course, be made adults-only with a splash of rum. The Cranberry Bourbon Sour on page 269 is a seasonal favorite of ours. And do you remember ice cream punches at holiday parties as a kid? I haven't seen them in decades, so I think it's time to bring them back! We've also included one of those: the Retro Sherbet Party Punch on page 263. Just thinking of that tangy sherbet floating on top of a sweet punch makes my mouth water!

I have given my all to this book to make sure that I've captured the best of the best when it comes to our holiday baking classics here on the Canadian Prairies. Even though this book is bursting with oodles of cakes, cookies, dainties, puddings, and dessert salads, I have an ever-present nagging urge to add just one more recipe to make it perfect. I could have included a solid 250 recipes if I had really run wild! (That's right, this is me reined in.) I've curated what I feel are the best of the best, what my family and I love to fill our home (and bellies) with.

I hope this book becomes the first one you pull out every year when starting your Christmas baking. I hope you find some new favorites and rediscover some forgotten treats you haven't made in years. And most of all, I hope you all have a very merry Christmas and happy holidays!

Love,
Karlynn

A VERY VINTAGE
CHRISTMAS

Christmas appeals to both my inner magpie (think of all the shiny decorations and sparkling lights) and my love of vintage (think of all the nostalgia attached to Christmas). Throughout this book, you'll see some of my very favorite vintage Christmas items I've collected, including the 1960s silver aluminum tree that I had wanted for as long as I can remember! I bought it for myself as my reward for sending in the finished manuscript and photos for my first cookbook, *Flapper Pie and a Blue Prairie Sky*, seven years ago. There's also the green aluminum tree I bought when I finished my second cookbook, *The Prairie Table*! Truth be told, as I'm writing this, I'm still trying to figure out where to fit another Christmas tree in the house . . . after all, this third book IS all about Christmas, right?

My aluminum trees are by no means the only vintage holiday dressings you'll see in this book. Almost every vintage decoration you'll see here has been thrifted or found at garage sales—I have been collecting for years! It's been so much fun having an excuse to hunt for Christmas treasures for the book. Beyond the fun, it's also led me through personal Christmas memories. The angel tree topper pictured with my Chocolate Bar Squares on page 199 is just like the one my Grandma Marion had on top of her Christmas tree. Finally, after searching for a long time, I found one while thrifting a few years back, and tears instantly welled up in my eyes as I remembered how I used to think she was the most beautiful angel I'd ever seen. I am still looking for the felt angel decorations Grandma Marion had on her tree. I can't wait until I finally find those as well!

Along with that magpie love of vintage items comes my well-known love of vintage recipes, and as far as a time for treasured recipes and thinking back on family gatherings gone by goes, nothing beats the holidays. True, every year some newer recipes make it into my repertoire (like my Mint Chocolate Dainties on page 169 and the Pumpkin Bread Pudding on page 244), but the recipes I just can't live without at Christmas are the ones my grandma and mom would make throughout my childhood. These old family recipes bring us closer together during the holidays, when we remember those who are no longer sitting at the table with us but remain close in our hearts. Every year, we serve my Grandma Marion's Christmas carrot pudding (page 240) for Christmas dessert, and while we eat, the conversation inevitably turns to stories of the many Christmases we spent out on her Manitoba farm. Stories like the time our car broke down just as we were trying to leave for our long drive home at 4 a.m. and we ended up having to stay an extra day. Have you ever tried getting your car fixed during the holidays in a small town? We had a miracle worker mechanic who came through for us. It could have been worse: we could have broken down in the middle of the lonely, freezing Prairies after leaving town that day! And then there was the time my sister brought home a puppy that my aunt's friend was giving away in Dauphin, Manitoba—only my sister would find a free puppy at Christmas and bring it home, I tell you. That dog (Oskar) was well loved and spoiled for 16 years after that Christmas.

These old family recipes bring us closer together during the holidays, when we remember those who are no longer sitting at the table with us but remain close in our hearts.

As you bake from this book, I hope the vintage recipes will bring back family memories, the new recipes will create new memories, and the Christmas decor will inspire extra Christmas spirit. Filled to the brim with as many festive decorations as I could possibly fit, this book is a feast for the eyes as well as for your holiday table!

CHRISTMAS COOKIE EXCHANGE

Nothing says Christmas like a cookie exchange! A time-honored tradition in the Prairies and beyond, a cookie exchange is the perfect way to help busy families during the holiday season. For those of you who are first-timers, a cookie exchange gives you the chance to try a bunch of new recipes for the holidays. There are two approaches you can take, depending on how many cookies you want to end up going home with (I get into that below), but either method leaves you well prepared for the season.

Not sure how to organize one? Here are my best tips and tricks for a stress-free and successful cookie exchange.

 Keep an eye out for the cookie tin icon in the book. These recipes make excellent exchange treats because they are either a big-batch recipe or are easy to double or triple to MAKE it a big batch.

THE STOCKING-YOUR-FRIENDS-UP COOKIE EXCHANGE

This classic type of cookie exchange is a lot more work for each guest, but everyone goes home with enough cookies to last them through the holiday season. Each guest brings one to two dozen of their cookie specialty for each guest, plus a dozen to sample at the gathering itself. The number of cookies to bake for the party depends on your personal preference and how much you want to send home with everyone, plus how many people are participating in the exchange. Guests should also send their recipes to the host ahead of time in case anyone wants a copy, and so the host can make sure there aren't any repeated recipes. After the event, the host can email out the recipes to those who want them.

With this type of exchange, it's usually easier to go nut-free, but if you don't, always keep the cookies with nuts away from the other cookies. The host prints out each recipe and places it with its cookie so that guests can read and see if it's safe given any allergies.

THE SAMPLING COOKIE EXCHANGE

This newer type of cookie exchange is popular as a more party-like event. Guests send their recipes to the host before the get-together (guests should also note if they have any allergies), then each guest bakes their own cookie recipe, bringing just enough cookies for everyone to try one. The host will make sure there aren't any duplicate recipes. Unlike the traditional cookie exchange, the purpose of the sampling exchange isn't to load up on cookies but to taste-test and take home new recipes to try yourself.

At the exchange, any cookies containing allergens should be kept separate from the others. Like with the stocking-your-friends-up exchange, the host prints out each recipe and places it with its cookie so that guests can see if it's safe given any allergies.

"RULES" FOR YOUR GUESTS

"Guidelines" is probably the better term to use than "rules," but either way, before you send out your invitations, it's best to outline what the event will entail for your guests. Here are my recommendations for an easy exchange:

* Each guest needs to send in their recipe to the host ahead of time so it can be shared at the party.
* For a stocking-up party, each guest should bring a minimum of one dozen cookies for each person. For a sampling party, each guest should bring enough cookies for everyone to taste-test one and take a couple home.
* Try not to have duplicate cookies. Whoever emails first gets dibs!
* Homemade is best, and only fair if everyone else is taking the time to do so!
* Nut-free is easiest, but if there are no allergies in your group, then it's up to you.
* Each guest should bring their own containers for taking their cookies home. If it's a stocking-up party, they need to bring a large enough container for dozens and dozens of cookies, or multiple containers if they prefer to keep them separate.
* If you're holding a larger, stocking-up exchange, the cookies need to freeze well for storage.

TIPS AND TRICKS FOR HOSTING

* Host the event early in December, or even in late November. The point is that it's stress-free, which may not be the case in the middle of the busy season!
* Serve a few savory snacks and remind guests not to eat before they arrive. You have to balance out all that sugar!
* Tea is nice at a cookie exchange, and so is Mr. Kitchen Magpie's Whisky Mulled Wine (page 269)!
* Have enough waxed paper or parchment paper on hand so your guests can use it to layer the cookies properly when they're packing them away.

* As the host, you can go the extra mile and offer cookie tins that you thrift, then pack up your cookies for your guests. You can even buy Christmas cookie tins at your local dollar store.
* Practice basic food and kitchen safety and hygiene at all times, and remind guests to wash their hands.

BAKING INGREDIENTS

HOLIDAY BAKING INGREDIENTS

While most baking ingredients are available year-round, there are more than a few ingredients in this book that only come out around Christmas or are scarce during the year, such as the mini gumdrops and the green candied cherries. Start looking early in the season and stock up when you can.

* **CANDIED GINGER:** This is a lovely addition to your baking, and while you can usually get it in stores year-round, it's something I like to make myself. See my recipe on page 253.
* **CANDIED MIXED PEELS:** These are cut-up candied lemon, orange, and citron peels that come in containers. Available year-round.
* **CANDY CANES:** You can get these online year-round, and they last forever, so I usually get them after Christmas while they're on sale and keep a stash for the following year.
* **CHERRIES, GLACE:** These are not maraschino cherries! They are red and green candied cherries that aren't in a syrup but are instead glazed with sticky sugar. Your best bet is to buy them at bulk stores, as they sell out fast in grocery stores around the holidays. Tip: The green always sells out faster than the red at the bulk stores. The red may be available year-round, but the green are not. These should show up in stores around November.
* **CHERRIES, MARASCHINO:** A classic! These come in a jar filled with syrup, and are available year-round.
* **CRANBERRIES:** Buy these fresh for the holidays. They are only available between October and December, so make sure you get them early in the fall, before they disappear from store shelves for another year, and bake with fresh cranberries while you can! You can freeze any remaining cranberries in a bag for later use.
* **DATES:** When it comes to using dates in my recipes, the ones that come chopped and packed up tightly in a plastic-covered block are the best, rather than the oiled whole ones in plastic containers, which won't stick together when baking. Available year-round.

* FLAVOR EXTRACTS: I'm going to tell you something that will save your sanity: buy mint and almond extracts in September. No matter what, one of these flavors (or both!) always ends up selling out close to Christmas. I make sure that I am ready to go with any and all extracts well before the holiday season.

* HOLIDAY CHOCOLATES: These types of treats, such as peppermint-flavored Hershey's Kisses, are only in stock once per year, starting near the beginning of fall, so be sure to stock up when you see them. Popular new flavors can sell out fast!

* MINCEMEAT: Sold in glass jars, mincemeat is typically available only around the holidays. In fact, some grocery stores stop carrying it once the holidays are over, so whenever you see it is the time to grab it!

* MINI GUMDROPS (BAKING FRUITLETS): Pictured with the Gumdrop Cookies on page 44, these are usually only available during the Christmas season. I buy and freeze them for the next year when I can.

* NONPAREILS: These tiny round balls made of sugar, like the rainbow ones pictured on the Gingerbread Cut-Out Cookies on page 67, are different from sprinkles, which come in all sorts of shapes and sizes. Available year-round.

* SANDING SUGAR: With crystals that are a larger grain than granulated sugar, sanding sugar is used for decorating and comes in a variety of colors. Available year-round.

* SASKATOON BERRIES: Used in my Saskatoon Perogies (page 20). We always freeze what we pick in the summer so we can enjoy them come wintertime. These are also known as serviceberries in the US. While readily available in the Prairie provinces, you can also buy them frozen from specialty stores in Canada, or simply substitute blueberries for a similar flavor.

* WHITE CHOCOLATE MELTING WAFERS: These are white chocolate disks sold at craft stores and bulk stores that melt much better than white chocolate chips do, which are prone to seizing.

CLASSIC BAKING INGREDIENTS

Now that you're set with holiday ingredients, let's talk general baking ingredients. Here are some specifications and advice that will help you achieve the best version of these recipes, and beyond! (My icing sugar tip, for example, is a must-read.)

* BAKING CHOCOLATE: The better the quality of chocolate you use, the better the quality of the treat.

* BAKING SODA AND POWDER: Always store in closed containers, as they both absorb moisture and odors from the air.

* BROWN SUGAR: Golden or light brown sugar is my standard.

* BUTTER: Always use unsalted unless I specify to use salted.

- COCOA POWDER: Use unsweetened Dutch-process cocoa powder, as natural cocoa powder is too acidic for these recipes as they're written.
- EGGS: Always use large eggs, and they should be at room temperature unless otherwise specified.
- FLOUR: All-purpose flour is the standard unless otherwise specified in the recipe.
- ICING SUGAR: Always use a fresh bag: once opened, the taste gets stale fast. Like baking soda, it also pulls odors from the surrounding items in the cupboard. Icing sugar is also known as powdered sugar or confectioner's sugar.
- LARD: Lard is the only way I was able to get my snickerdoodles on page 42 to be thick and fluffy. In other cookie recipes, you can use lard instead of butter for a softer cookie, but you lose that delicious butter flavor.
- MILK: Whole (3.25%) milk is best for these recipes.
- MOLASSES: Christmas baking tends to use cooking molasses (also called dark molasses) more than the other varieties, like fancy (also called light) or blackstrap, to achieve that truly dark molasses taste needed for gingerbread. The great thing is that each type has an easy substitute: if you like a lighter molasses flavor, simply sub in fancy molasses for the cooking molasses at a 1:1 replacement. If you'd rather a deeper molasses taste where a recipe calls for fancy, use cooking molasses instead.
- PEANUT BUTTER: I tend to stick with smooth, sugar-loaded peanut butter for my holiday baking, except when crunch is needed for texture. Natural peanut butter can have too much oil in it.
- SALT: Table salt is the standard unless otherwise specified.
- SPICES: Always store spices in closed bags or containers to keep them fresh. Ground spices lose their potency after two to three years. If they aren't as fragrant as they should be, purchase new spices.
- VANILLA: Although expensive, pure vanilla extract is worth it.

OUR UKRAINIAN CHRISTMAS FAVORITES

Our Ukrainian Christmas is very low-key compared to the traditional Orthodox Christmas celebrations, where families get together on January 6 to eat 12 courses of meatless dishes (meatless dishes are common for a religious fast before a big day; the amount represents the 12 apostles). But we do gather with my parents and siblings over a few favorite Ukrainian dishes.

Ukrainian Christmas is such an integral part of my family's holidays, I knew I had to include at least a few traditional recipes in my ultimate Christmas book! My second cookbook, *The Prairie Table*, has even more Ukrainian recipes, but these four dishes here are my favorites for the holidays and are the ones I usually make—thus, they are perfect to kick off this book's holiday extravaganza.

Kutia (page 18) is a sweet wheat berry soup that opens the meal. We don't make it every year, as it takes a couple of days to prepare and it's a 50/50 split in my family of people who actually like it, so for all the effort it takes, I need to have a really big craving for it or be in desperate need of a prosperous wheat harvest the next year (read the recipe and you'll understand what I mean).

Perogies are another must-include, and yes, I grew up enjoying this versatile dish as a dessert! Most people are familiar with a cheesy potato or bacon and sauerkraut filling, but I've included sweet, delicious Saskatoon Perogies (page 20) for you to try this Christmas. Boil them, fry them in salted butter until browned, and then sprinkle with sugar and serve with cream. I bet you'll love them.

Pampushky (page 22) are Ukrainian yeast doughnuts with prune filling (another traditional Ukrainian ingredient: prunes are in everything!), deep-fried to perfection. These are the ONLY doughnuts we make for Christmas, but let me tell you, that sweet dough is so good you can fill it with anything, any time of year.

And finally, khrustyky cookies, also known as angel wings, a traditional Ukrainian deep-fried cookie. What could be more Christmassy than a set of angel's wings?

~ KUTIA ~

Kutia is a traditional wheat berry dish served with Christmas Eve dinner—which for us means on December 24 and again for Epiphany Eve (Ukrainian Orthodox Christmas Eve) on January 6. Wheat symbolizes prosperity and luck, and there are many different traditions surrounding kutia, from leaving portions on the table after the meal for the souls of the deceased, to throwing it up to the ceiling and seeing how many grains stick as a prediction of next year's harvest prosperity. Another has the head of the family leaving a portion outside for Frost so that he'll leave next year's harvest alone and not ruin it. You'll need to start this dish a couple days ahead of serving to allow time to soak the wheat berries, process the poppy seeds, and then let the flavors blend in the fridge.

Makes 6 cups ❄ **Prep Time: 16 hours, including soaking** ❄
Total Time: 16 hours, 30 minutes plus chilling (if desired)

1½ cups wheat berries

½ cup poppy seeds

½ cup toasted sliced nuts (I like almonds, walnuts, or pecans; see tip, page 59)

½ cup raisins

½ cup milk

½ cup liquid honey

⅛ tsp salt

⅛ tsp ground cinnamon

1. Rinse the wheat berries until the water runs clear. Transfer to a bowl, add enough water to cover the berries by 2 to 3 inches, and soak overnight.

2. The next day, drain the berries and place in a medium saucepan with enough water to cover. Bring to a simmer, then cover and simmer over low heat for 3½ to 4 hours or until they are very tender and burst open on their own. Stir occasionally, adding more water if needed to keep the berries covered. Once the berries have softened, drain and transfer to a medium bowl.

3. Rinse the poppy seeds, then transfer to a medium saucepan with 2 cups water. Bring to a simmer and cook for 4 to 5 minutes.

4. Drain the poppy seeds, then transfer to a food processor and grind. Add to the bowl with the wheat berries.

5. Preheat the oven to 325°F.

6. In a small bowl, mix together the nuts, raisins, milk, and honey. Mix in the salt and cinnamon.

7. Pour the nut mixture over the wheat berry mixture and mix until combined. Spoon into a deep-dish pie plate, spreading evenly.

8. Bake, uncovered, for 25 to 30 minutes or until heated through and slightly thickened.

9. For the best flavor, let cool completely, then serve or cover with foil and refrigerate overnight or for up to 3 days.

SASKATOON PEROGIES

Once you try dessert perogies, there's no going back! Saskatoons are my favorite berry to use, but blueberries are a delicious substitute and available year-round. If you pick fresh saskatoons in the summer, freeze bagfuls so you can make these perogies year-round. If using frozen berries, thaw them on paper towels to absorb excess moisture.

Makes 9–10 dozen perogies ❄ **Prep Time: 1 hour, 30 minutes** ❄ **Total Time: 1 hour, 45 minutes plus rising**

½ cup unsalted butter, cubed

1 cup boiling water

1½ cups cold water

¾ cup instant potato flakes

¼ tsp salt

5 cups flour (approx.)

3–4 cups fresh saskatoon berries or blueberries, plus more for sprinkling (optional)

1 cup granulated sugar (approx.), plus more for sprinkling

3 Tbsp salted butter per 2 dozen perogies

Whipping cream or heavy cream, for serving

1. Place the unsalted butter in a large bowl. Pour the boiling water over it and stir until the butter is completely melted. Add the cold water and stir to combine. Stir in the potato flakes and salt until dissolved.

2. Stir in the flour until a soft, velvety dough forms. The dough will be slightly sticky, but you should be able to shake it off your hands easily. Add more flour if necessary.

3. Cover the bowl with plastic wrap, then drape a clean, dry tea towel over top and let rest in a warm, draft-free spot for 90 minutes.

4. Line two large baking sheets with parchment paper.

5. Divide the dough into 3 equal pieces. Keep the dough covered, but not refrigerated, when not working with it. It will lose its velvety texture if refrigerated, so plan to make all the perogies in the same day.

6. On a lightly floured work surface, roll out 1 piece of dough to ⅛-inch thickness. Using a 2½-inch cookie cutter (we use a clean empty soup can!), cut out as many circles as you can. Gather the scraps, roll out again, and cut more circles, repeating until all the dough from the first piece is used.

7. Place 4 or 5 berries (2 or 3 if they are large) in the center of each dough circle and sprinkle with ¼ teaspoon of the sugar. Fold the dough over into a half circle and pinch the edges together three or four times to ensure they are sealed. Place on a prepared baking sheet.

8. Repeat steps 6 and 7 with the remaining pieces of dough.

9. You can cook some perogies right away (see step 10), but for any you are freezing, put the baking sheets, uncovered, in the freezer for about 2 hours. Once the perogies are completely frozen,

transfer them to good-quality large freezer-safe plastic bags and freeze for up to 6 months. When you're ready to eat them, cook from frozen—do not thaw.

10. To cook the perogies, bring a large stockpot of water to a boil. Place 2 dozen perogies in the water, stirring to ensure they don't stick to the bottom. Once they start to float, boil them for 2 to 3 minutes (4 to 5 minutes from frozen) or until the dough puffs up slightly and the edges lose their raw look. (It's a myth that perogies are done as soon as they float—that's how you end up with raw dough!) Drain the perogies.

11. In a large skillet over medium-high heat, melt the salted butter. Add the perogies and fry for 5 minutes on each side or until browned on both sides.

12. Serve the perogies in a bowl with cream , a sprinkle of sugar, and additional berries, if desired.

PAMPUSHKY

These prune-filled doughnuts are one of my parents' favorite Ukrainian Christmas treats from child-hood! When I brought some over to my next-door neighbors, they destroyed every one within the night. While not everyone likes prune filling, this dough recipe makes the BEST filled doughnuts of any flavor! Simply replace the prune with your favorite pie filling. You can even play with what's in season—I'll be filling mine with saskatoon jam in the summer! *Recipe pictured on page 16.*

Makes 4 dozen doughnuts ❄ **Prep Time: 1 hour** ❄ **Total Time: 2 hours, 30 minutes plus rising**

Stand mixer with the paddle
  attachment

4 large baking sheets

YEAST STARTER

¼ cup warm water

1 Tbsp active dry ("traditional")
  yeast

½ tsp granulated sugar

DOUGH

1 cup milk

½ cup butter

¼ cup + 2 Tbsp granulated
  sugar

½ cup cold water

3 egg yolks

4¼ cups flour (approx.)

½ tsp salt

1. For the starter: Place all the starter ingredients in a small bowl and mix thoroughly with a spoon. Set aside.

2. For the dough: Place the milk, butter, and sugar in a large microwave-safe bowl or glass measuring cup and microwave on high power until the milk has scalded (it will be steamy and near to a boil), removing every 2 minutes to stir. This should take about 6 to 8 minutes total.

3. Transfer the milk mixture to the mixer bowl and, using a wooden spoon, stir in the cold water. Let cool.

4. Beat the egg yolks and add to the cooled milk mixture.

5. Check the yeast starter. Once it is bubbling, add to the milk mixture, attach the bowl to the mixer, and mix on low speed until well combined.

6. In a large bowl, whisk the flour with the salt.

7. Replace the paddle with the dough hook. With the mixer on its lowest speed, add 2 cups of the flour mixture. Gradually add the remaining flour mixture until the dough sticks to your hand very slightly but is still a solid, elastic dough. (Use up to ¼ cup more flour as necessary).

8. Transfer the dough to an oiled large bowl. Cover with a damp tea towel, place in a warm, draft-free area, and let rise until doubled in size, about 1 hour.

PRUNE FILLING

1 lb prunes, chopped

1 cup water

¼ cup granulated sugar

1 tsp lemon juice

Canola oil, for frying

Icing sugar, for dusting (optional)

9. For the filling: Meanwhile, place the prunes, water, and granulated sugar in a medium saucepan. Bring to a low boil and cook for 12 to 15 minutes or until a soft jam forms. Stir in the lemon juice, remove from the heat, and let cool.

10. Once the dough has doubled in size, punch it down in the bowl and divide into 4 equal pieces. Keep the dough covered when not working with it.

11. Butter two of the baking sheets.

12. Lightly flour a work surface. Working with 1 piece of dough at a time, divide it into 12 balls, then flatten each ball into a disk about 3 inches wide. Place a teaspoon of filling in the center of each disk. Be careful to keep the filling away from the edges or the dough may not seal properly. Fold the edges over the filling and pinch them together. Gently roll and form the dough into a ball, then place seam side down on a prepared baking sheet. Repeat with the remaining pieces of dough.

13. Cover the balls with a damp tea towel and let rise for 1 hour or until almost doubled in size.

14. In a deep fryer or a deep skillet, heat at least 3 inches of oil until it reaches 360°F on an instant-read thermometer. Line the other two baking sheets with paper towels.

15. Using a metal spatula, carefully lower the doughnuts into the hot oil, in batches of 3 or 4. Fry, turning with the spatula, until both sides are light golden brown, about 2 minutes per side. (Using the spatula helps keep the dough from deflating!) Using a slotted spoon, transfer the doughnuts to the paper towel–lined baking sheets. Repeat until you have fried all the doughnuts.

16. While the doughnuts are still hot, dust with icing sugar (if using). Let cool completely.

17. Store in an airtight container at room temperature for up to 3 days, or freeze solid on a parchment-lined baking sheet, then seal in freezer bags, removing as much air as possible, and freeze for up to 3 months.

KHRUSTYKY

Across different Eastern European cultures, the word "khrustyky" takes on various spellings, but these cookies are also commonly known as angel wings. The sweet sour cream dough is rolled thin, pulled into bowtie-like shapes, and then deep-fried to crispy perfection.

Makes 4 dozen cookies ❄ Prep Time: 40 minutes ❄ Total Time: 1 hour

2½ cups flour

1 tsp salt

6 egg yolks

¼ cup granulated sugar

½ cup sour cream

1 Tbsp vanilla extract

2 cups canola oil, for frying

1 cup icing sugar, for dusting

1. In a medium bowl, whisk together the flour and salt. Set aside.

2. In a stand mixer with the paddle attachment or in a large bowl using a handheld mixer, beat the egg yolks on medium speed until light and fluffy, about 2 minutes. With the mixer on low speed, gradually add the granulated sugar, beating constantly until the mixture is light and fluffy. Using a wooden spoon, stir in the sour cream and vanilla until fully incorporated.

3. Replace the mixer's paddle attachment or beaters with the dough hook. Add the flour mixture and knead on medium speed or by hand for about 5 minutes or until the dough no longer sticks to your fingers when you pull it off the hook.

4. On a lightly floured work surface, roll out the dough until extremely thin. The thinner the dough, the lighter and crispier the cookies will be. Cut the dough into strips that are 4 to 5 inches long and 1 inch wide.

5. To make a loop or bow, cut a lengthwise 1-inch slit in the center of a dough strip. Thread one end through the hole, gently pulling it through until the dough has twisted into a bowtie shape. (This takes practice.) Repeat with the remaining dough strips.

6. In a deep fryer or a large, heavy-bottomed skillet, heat the oil until it reaches 360°F on an instant-read thermometer. Line two large baking sheets with paper towels.

7. Using a slotted spoon, place 1 cookie at a time in the oil, in batches of 5 or 6. Fry for 30 to 45 seconds, turning once to brown both sides. Transfer to the prepared baking sheet to drain. Repeat until you have fried all the cookies.

8. While the cookies are still hot, dust the cookies with the icing sugar, using a sifter or sieve. Store in an airtight container in layers, with parchment or waxed paper between each layer, at room temperature for up to 5 days or in the freezer for up to 3 months.

CHAPTER ONE

SHORTBREAD & SUGAR COOKIES

P latters of beautiful treats, baking days with the kids, leaving out whipped shortbread for Santa . . . is it any wonder that nothing seems to be more synonymous with Christmas baking than the cookie?

Christmas cookies remind me of my kids. I have a video of my son when he was three years old "helping" me make whipped shortbread. He was standing at the counter on a chair, picking off and eating all the cherries as soon as I'd placed them on the unbaked dough. He had these adorable little chipmunk cheeks, full of candied cherries. Now he's an adult and, at six foot four, he's reaching way up for the top-shelf ingredients for his mom.

Shortbread is such a staple that I have five different types to start out this chapter, each the perfect Christmas cookie in its own way. How you'd be able to choose just one I'm not sure, but you can have lots of fun taste-testing! My new top treat is the maple shortbread on page 32, but nothing will ever replace whipped shortbread (page 28) as THE Christmas cookie for my family.

And, of course, sugar cookies are great for making with kids. I had a friend test the Stained Glass Window Cookies (page 54) with her six-year-old son, and they were duly amazed at how beautiful they turned out. Of course, not everything turns out beautifully! You'll notice in the photos for the Cut-Out Sugar Cookies (page 56) that my icing decorations are not picture-perfect. I made those with my kids, and I treasure them far more than any photo-worthy cookies I could make by sitting down alone to decorate for hours. I want messy, mismatched cookies that we pull out of the cookie jar and laugh at later, trying to remember who decorated which.

Cookies really are the best for exchanges and gifting: they're easy to make and pack up, and they freeze well, so they can be made a few months ahead. Always freeze cookies in layers, with waxed paper or parchment paper between each layer, in an airtight container.

Traditional Whipped Shortbread

Whipped shortbread is THE Christmas cookie in my household, so even though it made an appearance in *Flapper Pie and a Blue Prairie Sky*, you'll understand why I had to bring it back for another round! It's the one the kids left out for Santa every Christmas, the one everyone anticipated in my yearly Christmas baking basket, and the one that reminds me of my Grandma Marion the most. This was her favorite Christmas cookie, and she made it every Christmas, without fail.

Makes 2 dozen cookies ❄ **Prep Time: 40 minutes** ❄ **Total Time: 1 hour, 50 minutes**

1 cup salted butter, softened

½ cup icing sugar

1½ cups flour

Glace cherries, for topping (optional)

1. Preheat the oven to 275°F.

2. In a stand mixer with the paddle attachment or in a large bowl using a handheld mixer, beat together the butter and icing sugar on medium speed until light and fluffy. With the mixer on low speed, gradually add the flour, mixing until fully incorporated. Beat on medium speed for 6 minutes, scraping the sides and bottom of the bowl with a spatula every 2 minutes.

3. Using a tablespoon-sized cookie scoop, scoop dough balls onto two ungreased large baking sheets, spacing them 2 inches apart. Top each scoop with a cherry (if using).

4. Bake, one sheet at a time, for 30 to 35 minutes or until the bottoms are nicely browned. Carefully transfer the cookies to wire racks to cool completely.

5. Store in an airtight container in layers, with parchment or waxed paper between each layer, at room temperature for up to 5 days or in the freezer for up to 3 months.

SCOTTISH SHORTBREAD

Every Christmas, Mr. Kitchen Magpie reminisces about how his Scottish grandma used to make the most delicious, crispy, buttery shortbread. When he first waxed poetic about how delicious it was, I wasn't buying it—my whipped shortbread (page 28) is the only one I would even consider baking. I'm a bit of shortbread snob, it seems. That said, I gave his grandma's recipe a whirl, using brown sugar for flavor and icing sugar for texture, and now I'm a believer. Nothing beats this shortbread paired with a hot cup of tea. Scottish shortbread is traditionally cut into circles and rectangles with serrated edges, then baked thin to get that signature buttery, crispy snap.

Makes 2–3 dozen cookies ❉ Prep Time: 25 minutes ❉ Total Time: 1 hour

2 cups flour

½ tsp salt

1 cup butter, softened

¼ cup packed brown sugar

¼ cup icing sugar

1. Preheat the oven to 350°F. Line two baking sheets with parchment paper.

2. In a medium bowl, whisk together the flour and salt. Set aside.

3. In a stand mixer with the paddle attachment or in a large bowl using a handheld mixer, beat the butter and brown sugar on medium speed until smooth. Beat in the icing sugar until smooth. With the mixer on low speed (this is not whipped shortbread, after all), gradually add the flour mixture, mixing until fully incorporated.

4. On a lightly floured work surface, roll out the dough to ¼-inch thickness. Cut into shapes as desired. (Using a cookie cutter with a serrated edges yields crispy, snappy cookie edges that can't be beat.) Reroll the scraps and continue to cut cookies until all the dough is used.

5. Place the cookies on the prepared baking sheets, spacing them 2 inches apart. (You may need to set some aside for a third batch.) Pierce the top of each cookie with a fork two or three times to help them vent steam while baking.

6. Bake, one sheet at a time, for 10 to 12 minutes or until the bottoms are lightly browned. Let cool on the baking sheet for 5 minutes, then transfer the cookies to wire racks to cool completely.

7. Store in an airtight container in layers, with parchment or waxed paper between each layer, at room temperature for up to 5 days or in the freezer for up to 3 months.

BAKING TIP: Make sure there are no lumps in your brown sugar, as these won't melt when baked and can lead to lumps in your cookies.

Maple Meltaway Shortbread Cookies

These are the ultimate shortbread cookies if you love maple and pecan flavors! Make sure you get an excellent-quality maple extract: the better it tastes, the better your cookies will taste. If you're a fan of the classic pairing of maple and walnut, feel free to use walnuts instead of chopped pecans.

Makes 3 dozen cookies ❄ **Prep Time: 20 minutes** ❄ **Total Time: 1 hour, 5 minutes**

1 cup salted butter, softened

½ cup icing sugar

1½ tsp maple extract

2 cups flour

½ cup finely chopped pecans

36 pecan halves, for topping

1. Preheat the oven to 350°F. Line two baking sheets with parchment paper.

2. In a stand mixer with the paddle attachment or in a medium bowl using a handheld mixer, beat the butter and icing sugar on medium speed until light and fluffy. Beat in the maple extract until combined. With the mixer on low speed, gradually add the flour, mixing until a soft dough forms. Beat on medium speed for 1 minute. Using a wooden spoon, stir in the chopped pecans until evenly distributed.

3. Using a tablespoon-sized cookie scoop, scoop dough balls onto the prepared baking sheets, spacing them 2 inches apart. (You will need to set some dough aside for a third batch.) Gently press a pecan half into the top of each cookie.

4. Bake, one sheet at a time, for 14 to 15 minutes or until the bottoms are lightly browned and the cookies are dried out. Let cool on the baking sheet for 5 minutes, then transfer the cookies to wire racks to cool completely.

5. Store in an airtight container in layers, with parchment or waxed paper between each layer, at room temperature for up to 5 days or in the freezer for up to 3 months.

CHOCOLATE SHORTBREAD

The crispy, buttery snap of classic Scottish shortbread is elevated to total decadence here with the addition of cocoa. My theory that adding chocolate makes everything better proved true with these cookies! Chocolate shortbread makes the perfect treat for your cookie exchange, and the perfect pairing with your Christmas morning coffee. The pinch of cinnamon is optional but really boosts the chocolate flavor.

Makes 5 dozen cookies ❄ **Prep Time: 20 minutes** ❄ **Total Time: 1 hour, 20 minutes**

1½-inch square or round cookie cutter (or both!)

1½ cups salted butter, softened

¾ cup icing sugar

½ cup unsweetened cocoa powder

2 cups flour

Pinch of ground cinnamon (optional)

1. Preheat the oven to 350°F. Line two baking sheets with parchment paper.

2. In a stand mixer with the paddle attachment or in a large bowl using a handheld mixer, beat the butter and icing sugar on high speed until smooth. Beat in the cocoa until fully incorporated. With the mixer on low speed, gradually add the flour and cinnamon (if using), mixing until fully incorporated.

3. On a lightly floured work surface, roll out the dough to ¼-inch thickness. Using the cookie cutter, and rerolling the scraps as needed, cut out 60 cookies. Place on the prepared baking sheets, spacing them 2 inches apart. (You will need to set some aside for further batches.) Pierce the top of each cookie with a fork two or three times to help them vent steam while baking.

4. Bake, one sheet at a time, for 10 to 12 minutes or until the edges are set. Let cool on the baking sheet for 5 minutes, then transfer the cookies to wire racks to cool completely.

5. Store in an airtight container in layers, with parchment or waxed paper between each layer, at room temperature for up to 5 days or in the freezer for up to 3 months.

TIP:

These cookies can also be cut into shapes to decorate, like my sugar cookies with royal icing on page 56.

Icebox Shortbread Cookies

These versatile beauties can be made as cookies or as squares. The choice of mix-ins is up to you—you can try chocolate chips, toffee bits, chopped nuts, or cranberries—but my favorite is the pistachio-cranberry combination shown in the photo! These cookies are best when baked to a buttery, crunchy crisp like a shortbread, but can be underbaked if you prefer a soft cookie.

Makes 3 dozen cookies ✳ Prep Time: 20 minutes ✳ Total Time: 1 hour, 10 minutes plus chilling for rolled cookies; 1 hour, 35 minutes plus chilling for sliced squares

2 cups flour

½ tsp salt

1 cup butter, softened

¼ cup packed brown sugar

¼ cup icing sugar

1 egg yolk

½ tsp vanilla extract

1 cup mix-ins (such as chocolate chips, toffee bits, chopped nuts, sweetened dried cranberries, and/or pistachios)

1 cup toppings (such as sprinkles or halved glace cherries, optional)

BASIC ICEBOX DOUGH

1. In a medium bowl, whisk together the flour and salt. Set aside.

2. In a stand mixer with the paddle attachment or in a large bowl using a handheld mixer, beat the butter, brown sugar, and icing sugar on medium speed until light and fluffy. Add the egg yolk, beating well. Mix in the vanilla on low speed until combined. With the mixer on low speed (after all, this is not whipped shortbread), gradually add the flour mixture, mixing until fully incorporated. Using a wooden spoon, stir in your chosen mix-ins until evenly distributed. Follow the method for cookies or squares.

ROLLED COOKIES

1. Divide the dough into 2 equal pieces and roll each into a log about 6 inches long and 1½ inches in diameter. Wrap tightly with waxed paper, pressing to remove any air pockets. Refrigerate for 1 hour or until very firm.

2. Preheat the oven to 325°F. Line two large baking sheets with parchment paper.

3. Remove the waxed paper from the dough. Using a serrated knife, slice each log into eighteen ⅓-inch-thick circles. Place on the prepared baking sheets, spacing them 2 inches apart. (You will need to set some aside for a third batch.)

4. Bake, one sheet at a time, for 15 to 16 minutes or until the cookies are lightly browned and dried out. (For softer cookies, reduce the baking time by 2 to 3 minutes.) Let cool on the baking sheet for 5 minutes, then transfer the cookies to wire racks to cool completely.

see over

5. Store in an airtight container in layers, with parchment or waxed paper between each layer, at room temperature for up to 5 days or in the freezer for up to 3 months.

SLICED SQUARES

1. Line a 9-inch square pan with waxed or parchment paper. Turn out the dough into the pan and pat into an even layer in the bottom. Refrigerate for 1 hour or until very firm.

2. Preheat the oven to 325°F. Line two large baking sheets with parchment paper.

3. Cut the shortbread into 36 squares. Place on the prepared baking sheets, spacing them 2 inches apart. (You will need to set some aside for a third batch.) Add the toppings (if using) to each square (a halved glace cherry works perfectly).

4. Bake, one sheet at a time, for 20 to 25 minutes or until the squares are lightly browned and dried out. (For softer squares, reduce the baking time by 3 to 4 minutes.) Let cool on the baking sheet for 5 minutes, then transfer the squares to wire racks to cool completely.

5. Store in an airtight container in layers, with parchment or waxed paper between each layer, at room temperature for up to 5 days or in the freezer for up to 3 months.

THIN & CHEWY SNICKERDOODLES

These thin, chewy snickerdoodles were one the most popular cookie recipes from my first book, *Flapper Pie and a Blue Prairie* Sky—they are a true classic, and you simply can't leave snickerdoodles out of a Christmas baking book! For those who prefer thicker, more cake-like snickerdoodles, I've also included a new recipe on page 42.

Makes 4 dozen cookies ❄ **Prep Time: 20 minutes** ❄ **Total Time: 1 hour**

3½ cups flour

3 tsp cream of tartar

1⅓ tsp baking soda

¼ tsp salt

1½ cups butter, softened

2¼ cups + ⅓ cup granulated sugar, divided

3 eggs

1½ tsp vanilla extract

1 tsp ground cinnamon

1. Preheat the oven to 375°F. Line two baking sheets with parchment paper.

2. In a medium bowl, whisk together the flour, cream of tartar, baking soda, and salt. Set aside.

3. In a stand mixer with the paddle attachment or in a large bowl using a handheld mixer, beat together the butter and 2¼ cups of the sugar on medium speed until smooth and creamy. Add the eggs, one at a time, beating well after each. Mix in the vanilla until combined. With the mixer on low speed, gradually add the flour mixture, mixing until a smooth dough forms.

4. In a small bowl, combine the remaining ⅓ cup sugar and cinnamon. For each cookie, roll a tablespoon of dough into a ball, then roll in the sugar mixture to coat. Place on the prepared baking sheets, spacing them 2 inches apart. (You will need to set some aside for further batches.)

5. Bake, one sheet at a time, for 8 to 10 minutes or until the bottoms are browned. Let cool on the baking sheet for 2 to 3 minutes, then transfer the cookies to wire racks to cool completely.

6. Store in an airtight container in layers, with parchment or waxed paper between each layer, at room temperature for up to 5 days or in the freezer for up to 3 months.

Thick & Puffy Snickerdoodles

It took me nearly a decade to finally admit that thick, monstrous snickerdoodle cookies like the ones I admire at Disneyland are just never going to happen with butter. Those commercial cookies use vegetable shortening, I'm sure—something I avoid in my baking because hydrogenated oils contain high levels of trans fat. Now lard, on the other hand . . . well, it turns out that pork lard makes wonderfully thick and cakey snickerdoodles that are perfect for leaving out for Santa!

Makes 3 dozen cookies ❄ Prep Time: 20 minutes ❄ Total Time: 1 hour plus chilling

2¾ cups sifted flour

2 tsp cream of tartar

1 tsp baking soda

½ tsp salt

1 cup lard

1½ cups + ⅓ cup granulated sugar

1 egg

2 egg yolks

2 tsp vanilla extract

1 Tbsp ground cinnamon

1. In a medium bowl, whisk together the flour, cream of tartar, baking soda, and salt. Set aside.

2. In a stand mixer with the paddle attachment or in a large bowl using a handheld mixer, beat the lard and 1½ cups sugar on medium speed until combined. Add the egg and egg yolks, one at a time, beating well after each. Mix in the vanilla until combined. With the mixer on low speed, gradually add the flour mixture, mixing until fully incorporated.

3. Cover the bowl with plastic wrap and refrigerate for at least 1 hour or for up to 3 days.

4. Preheat the oven to 400°F. Line two baking sheets with parchment paper.

5. Combine the remaining ⅓ sugar and cinnamon in a small bowl. Roll the dough into balls the size of golf balls, then roll each in the sugar mixture. Place on the baking sheets, spacing them 2 inches apart. (You will need to set some aside for a third batch.)

6. Bake, one sheet at a time, for 10 to 12 minutes or until lightly browned with cracked tops. Do not overbake or they will be dry. Let cool completely on the baking sheets.

7. Store in an airtight container in layers, with parchment or waxed paper between each layer, at room temperature for up to 5 days or in the freezer for up to 3 months.

GUMDROP COOKIES

These are a chewy jawbreaker of a cookie meant for gumdrop lovers! There is just something so festive about these brightly colored cookies. The mini gumdrops that work best (see the photo opposite) are among those goodies that stores stock leading up to Christmas. But if you're unable to find them, you can use standard-sized gumdrops and chop them into smaller pieces. If I'm not finding the minis in abundance, I usually stock up on a couple of bags to freeze for the following year!

Makes 2 dozen cookies ❄ Prep Time: 20 minutes ❄ Total Time: 50 minutes

1¾ cups flour

½ tsp baking soda

½ tsp salt

½ cup butter, softened

1 cup granulated sugar

1 egg

½ tsp almond extract

1 cup fruit-flavored mini gumdrops (or chopped standard-sized gumdrops)

1. Preheat the oven to 350°F. Line two large baking sheets with parchment paper.

2. In a medium bowl, whisk together the flour, baking soda, and salt. Set aside.

3. In a stand mixer with the paddle attachment or in a large bowl using a handheld mixer, beat the butter and sugar on high speed until smooth and creamy. Add the egg, beating well. Mix in the almond extract until combined. With the mixer on low speed, gradually add the flour mixture, mixing until fully incorporated. Using a wooden spoon, stir in the gumdrops until evenly distributed.

4. Using a tablespoon-sized cookie scoop, scoop dough balls onto the prepared baking sheets, spacing them about 2 inches apart.

5. Bake, one sheet at a time, for 12 to 15 minutes or until golden brown. Let cool on the baking sheet for 2 to 3 minutes, then transfer the cookies to wire racks to cool completely.

6. Store in an airtight container in layers, with parchment or waxed paper between each layer, at room temperature for up to 5 days or in the freezer for up to 3 months.

BAKING TIP:
If you find that your cookies spread too much while baking, next time try refrigerating the dough for an hour beforehand.

Pinwheel Cookies

Nothing is more fun for a kid at Christmas than red-and-green pinwheel cookies! While that version was definitely a childhood favorite of mine, I've grown to love a fruit filling as an adult. The dough recipe can be used to make any type of pinwheel cookie—I've included recipes for my favorite fruit fillings, as well as a festively colored version. You can color the festive version's dough however you want, or even switch the vanilla flavoring for mint or raspberry.

Makes 40–60 cookies ❄ **Prep Time: 30 minutes** ❄ **Total Time: 1 hour, 20 minutes plus chilling**

4 cups flour

½ tsp baking powder

½ tsp salt

1 cup butter, softened

1 cup granulated sugar

1 cup packed brown sugar

2 eggs

3 tsp vanilla, mint, or raspberry extract

Filling of choice (for Classic Version, see page 48)

¼ tsp red food coloring (for Festive Version)

¼ tsp green food coloring (for Festive Version)

DOUGH & BAKING

1. For the dough, in a medium bowl, whisk together the flour, baking powder, and salt. Set aside.

2. In a stand mixer with the paddle attachment or in a large bowl using a handheld mixer, beat the butter, granulated sugar, and brown sugar on medium speed until light and fluffy. Add the eggs, one at a time, beating until fully incorporated. Mix in the extract until combined. With the mixer on low speed, gradually add the flour mixture, mixing until fully incorporated. The dough should be dry but still stick together.

3. To make your favorite flavor of pinwheel cookie, follow the method for either the Classic or Festive Version (see page 48), then return to step 4 to bake.

4. To bake, preheat the oven to 350°F. Line two large baking sheets with parchment paper.

5. Remove the wrapping and cut each log into twenty ½-inch-thick circles. Place on the prepared baking sheets, spacing them 2 inches apart. (If baking more than one log, you will need to set some dough aside for further batches.)

6. Bake, one sheet at a time, for 9 to 10 minutes or until set. Be careful not to brown these cookies (they brown quickly). Let cool on the baking sheet for 5 minutes, then transfer the cookies to wire racks to cool completely.

7. Store in an airtight container in layers, with parchment or waxed paper between each layer, at room temperature for up to 5 days or in the freezer for up to 3 months.

see over

CLASSIC VERSION

1. Divide the dough into 3 equal pieces and shape each into a disk. Wrap each disk tightly with plastic wrap and refrigerate for 1 hour or until firm enough to roll.

2. To prepare the pinwheels, roll out each disk between two sheets of waxed or parchment paper into a 10-inch square about ¼ inch thick (keeping any disk you're not working on in the fridge). Remove the top sheet of paper. Spread a third of the filling over top in an even layer, leaving a ½-inch border around the edges. Roll up the dough tightly into a log, cinnamon bun–style. Keeping the end firmly tucked under, wrap tightly with plastic wrap. Repeat with the remaining dough and filling. Refrigerate until very firm, or the dough won't slice properly. To freeze for later, place the wrapped logs in freezer bags and freeze for up to 3 months. Thaw in the fridge, then continue with step 4 in the main method to bake.

FESTIVE VERSION

1. Divide the dough into 2 equal pieces. Return 1 portion to the bowl, add the red food coloring, and beat on low speed until incorporated and uniform in color. Divide the red dough into 2 equal pieces and shape each into a disk. Wrap each disk tightly with plastic wrap and refrigerate for 1 hour or until firm enough to roll.

2. Clean the bowl and beaters of all red dough, then place the remaining dough portion in the bowl. Add the green food coloring and beat on low speed until incorporated and uniform in color. Divide the green dough into 2 equal pieces and shape each into a disk. Wrap each disk tightly with plastic wrap and refrigerate for 1 hour or until firm enough to roll.

3. To prepare the pinwheels, roll out a red disk between two sheets of waxed or parchment paper into a 10-inch square about ¼ inch thick. Repeat with a green disk. Remove the top sheet of paper. Flip the green dough over on top of the red dough, matching up the square edges, then gently remove the paper. Trim the edges so that the doughs match up. Roll up the dough tightly into a log, cinnamon bun–style. Keeping the end firmly tucked under, wrap tightly with plastic wrap. Repeat with the remaining red and green disks. Refrigerate until very firm, or the dough won't slice properly. To freeze for later, place the wrapped logs in freezer bags and freeze for up to 3 months. Thaw in the fridge, then continue with step 4 in the main method to bake.

Pinwheel Cookie Fillings

Here are some of my favorite fillings to use for the pinwheel cookies. Remember that each recipe gets divided into three: one-third for each disk of dough. For example, for the raspberry walnut filling, you'd use 1/3 cup raspberry jam and 1/3 cup chopped walnuts on one disk of dough.

RASPBERRY WALNUT FILLING

1 cup raspberry jam

1 cup finely chopped walnuts

1. In a small bowl, combine the jam and walnuts.
2. Use as directed in step 2 of the classic pinwheel version (page 48).

MINCEMEAT FILLING

1 cup canned mincemeat

1. Use as directed in step 2 of the classic pinwheel version (page 48).

APRICOT FILLING

1½ cups finely chopped dried apricots

⅔ cup water (approx.)

1 cup finely chopped pecans (optional)

1. In a large saucepan, combine the apricots and water. Bring to a low boil. Reduce the heat and simmer for 15 to 20 minutes or until the mixture has thickened and the apricots have softened. If the apricots aren't soft enough, add a bit more water and continue to simmer until the mixture thickens and resembles jam.
2. Remove from the heat and stir in the pecans (if using) until evenly distributed. Let cool completely.
3. Use as directed in step 2 of the classic pinwheel version (page 48).

DATE FILLING

2 cups chopped dates

½ cup granulated sugar

½ cup water (approx.)

1. In a large saucepan, combine the dates, sugar, and water. Bring to a low boil. Reduce the heat and simmer for 15 to 20 minutes or until the mixture has thickened and the dates have softened. If the dates aren't soft enough, add a bit more water and continue to simmer until the mixture thickens and resembles jam. Let cool completely.
2. Use as directed in step 2 of the classic pinwheel version (page 48).

THUMBPRINT COOKIES

My favorite combination for thumbprint cookies is the classic: walnuts with raspberry jam. However, this base recipe is easy for you to customize to your liking. My mom doesn't have a crazy sweet tooth like the rest of the family, but the raspberry-walnut combination is the one cookie I remember her baking for herself to enjoy every Christmas when I was a kid in the '80s. (She did share, of course.)

Makes 3 dozen cookies ❄ **Prep Time: 20 minutes** ❄ **Total Time: 1 hour, 15 minutes plus chilling**

2 cups flour

¼ cup icing sugar

½ tsp salt

1 cup butter, softened

½ cup packed brown sugar

2 eggs, separated

½ tsp vanilla extract

¾ cup finely chopped walnuts or other nuts of choice (optional)

¾ cup raspberry jam or other jam of choice

1. In a medium bowl, whisk together the flour, icing sugar, and salt. Set aside.

2. In a stand mixer with the paddle attachment or in a large bowl using a handheld mixer, beat the butter and brown sugar on high speed until smooth and creamy, about 2 minutes. Add the egg yolks, beating well. Mix in the vanilla until combined. With the mixer on low speed, gradually add the flour mixture, mixing until fully incorporated.

3. Cover the bowl with plastic wrap and refrigerate for 1 hour.

4. Preheat the oven to 325°F. Line two large baking sheets with parchment paper.

5. If using nuts, place them in a small bowl.

6. In a medium bowl, lightly beat the egg whites until frothy.

7. For each cookie, roll a tablespoonful of dough into a ball, then dip in the egg whites and roll in the nuts. Place on a prepared baking sheet. Press an indent into the top, and fill the indent with jam. Repeat with the remaining dough, spacing the balls 2 inches apart. (You will need to set some aside for a third batch.)

8. Bake, one sheet at a time, for 15 to 18 minutes or until the cookies are golden brown (if using nuts, they should be toasted and browned). Transfer the cookies to wire racks to cool completely.

9. Store in an airtight container in layers, with parchment or waxed paper between each layer, at room temperature for up to 5 days or in the freezer for up to 3 months.

Classic Spritz Cookies

This dough is meant to be used in a cookie press, whether brand new or vintage from a thrift store—start looking before Christmas, when people donate them to declutter (see tip). The dough consistency for a cookie press has to be just right, not really airy like my whipped shortbread, but not so thick that it won't go through the press. The trick is to make sure the dough is cold; otherwise, it will get stuck when you're trying to dispense your swirls, trees, or other shapes. When this happens to me, I stick the entire cookie press full of dough in the fridge for 20 minutes—then I'm back to pressing, no problem.

Makes 3 dozen cookies ❄ Prep Time: 20 minutes ❄ Total Time: 1 hour plus chilling

Cookie press with assorted
  shape plates

2½ cups flour

½ tsp salt

1 cup butter, softened

⅔ cup granulated sugar

1 egg

1 tsp vanilla extract

Crushed peppermint candies,
  sanding sugar, sprinkles, or
  nuts, for decoration

TIP:
Try to find one that
is all metal, as these
chill much better
than the newer
plastic ones, and
the dough doesn't
stick as much.

1. In a medium bowl, whisk together the flour and salt. Set aside.

2. In a stand mixer with the paddle attachment or in a large bowl using a handheld mixer, beat the butter and sugar on high speed until smooth and creamy, about 2 minutes. Add the egg, beating well. Mix in the vanilla until combined. With the mixer on low speed, gradually add the flour mixture, mixing until fully incorporated.

3. If the dough is so sticky that it clings to your hands when touched, refrigerate for up to 1 hour. It needs to be firm, yet able to pipe through the press. Sticky dough will stick in the press! As you press cookies in step 5, keep dough you're not currently working with in the fridge.

4. Preheat the oven to 350°F. Line two baking sheets with parchment paper.

5. Fill the cookie press with dough and stamp the shapes onto the prepared baking sheets, spacing them 2 inches apart. (You will need to set some aside for a third batch.) Decorate the cookies as desired.

6. Bake, one sheet at a time, for 8 to 10 minutes or until set but not brown. Immediately transfer the cookies to wire racks to cool completely.

7. Store in an airtight container in layers, with parchment or waxed paper between each layer, at room temperature for up to 5 days or in the freezer for up to 3 months.

STAINED GLASS WINDOW COOKIES

This recipe is a classic to make with kids for a reason. Not only is it fun to smash the candies and watch the middles melt in the oven, but you can also thread a ribbon through the cookies and place them on the tree as pretty homemade ornaments. However, I don't advise this if you have pets. (I don't need to get into how I know this, but I can tell you it wasn't the dog who was the troublemaker in this instance.)

Makes 2–3 dozen cookies ❄ **Prep Time: 50 minutes** ❄ **Total Time: 1 hour, 35 minutes plus chilling**

2 cookie cutters of the same shape, in two different sizes

2¼ cups flour (approx.)

⅓ cup icing sugar

½ tsp baking powder

½ tsp salt

¾ cup butter, softened

¾ cup granulated sugar

1 egg

2 tsp vanilla extract

30–40 clear hard candies in various colors

1. In a medium bowl, whisk together the flour, icing sugar, baking powder, and salt. Set aside.

2. In a stand mixer with the paddle attachment or in a large bowl using a handheld mixer, beat the butter and granulated sugar on high speed until smooth and creamy, about 2 minutes. Add the egg, beating well. Mix in the vanilla until combined. With the mixer on low speed, gradually add the flour mixture, mixing until fully incorporated. If the dough sticks to your hands when touched, mix in another tablespoon of flour.

3. Divide the dough into 2 equal pieces and shape each into a disk. Wrap each disk tightly with plastic wrap and refrigerate for at least 3 hours or for up to 3 days.

4. Sort the candies by color into separate small zip-top bags. Use a rolling pin or meat mallet to smash the candies into tiny pieces.

5. Preheat the oven to 350°F. Line two baking sheets with parchment paper.

6. On a lightly floured work surface, roll out each disk of dough to ¼-inch thickness (keeping the second disk in the fridge), rotating it 90 degrees after each roll to prevent sticking. Use more flour as needed to prevent stickiness. Using the larger cookie cutter, cut out cookies and place them on the prepared baking sheets, spacing them 2 inches apart. Reroll the scraps and continue to cut out cookies until all the dough is used.

7. Using the smaller cookie cutter, cut out the center of each cookie. Reroll the centers, cutting more large cookies. Repeat until the

sheets are full. (You may need to set some dough aside for a third batch; refrigerate it until you cut the next batch.)

8. Fill the center of each cookie three-quarters full with crushed candies in one color, alternating colors with each cookie.

9. Bake, one sheet at a time, for 12 to 14 minutes or until the candies have melted into pools in the middle of the cookies and the cookie tops are lightly browned. Let cool completely on the baking sheets.

10. Store in an airtight container in layers, with parchment or waxed paper between each layer, at room temperature for up to 5 days or in the freezer for up to 3 months.

Cut-Out Sugar Cookies

These sugar cookies manage to be soft and chewy, yet still hold their shape even when rolled out and cut into shapes. With their versatility, they are good for any holiday!

Makes 4 dozen cookies ❄ **Prep Time: 20 minutes** ❄ **Total Time: 1 hour, 5 minutes plus chilling**

4½ cups flour (approx.)

1 cup icing sugar

1 tsp baking powder

1 tsp salt

1½ cups butter, softened

1¼ cups granulated sugar

3 eggs

1 Tbsp vanilla extract

½ tsp almond extract

Royal Icing (page 250), for decorating

Sprinkles, for decorating

TIP:

For a lemon version, use lemon extract instead of almond, and add the zest of 1 lemon with the extract. It's a fabulous change of flavor!

1. In a medium bowl, whisk together the flour, icing sugar, baking powder, and salt. Set aside.

2. In a stand mixer with the paddle attachment or in a large bowl using a handheld mixer, beat the butter and granulated sugar on high speed until smooth and creamy, about 2 minutes. Add the eggs, one at a time, beating well after each. Add the vanilla and almond extract; stir to combine. With the mixer on low speed, gradually add the flour mixture, mixing until fully incorporated. If the dough is too sticky to roll out, add a tablespoon of flour.

3. Divide the dough into 4 equal pieces and shape each into a disk. Wrap each disk tightly with plastic wrap and refrigerate for at least 3 hours or for up to 3 days.

4. Preheat the oven to 350°F. Line two baking sheets with parchment paper.

5. On a lightly floured work surface, roll out each disk to ¼-inch thickness, rotating it 90 degrees after each roll to prevent sticking (keeping any disk you're not working on in the fridge). Use more flour as needed to prevent stickiness. Using a cookie cutter, and rerolling the scraps as needed, cut out 48 cookies. Place on the prepared baking sheets, spacing them 2 inches apart. (You will need to set some aside for further batches.)

6. Bake, one sheet at a time, for 10 to 11 minutes or until the cookies have only just browned on the edges and have lost their shine—the dough will look dull and the cookies will be firm. Let cool on the baking sheet for 5 minutes, then transfer the cookies to wire racks to cool completely.

7. Decorate the cookies with the royal icing, then sprinkles. Let set until dry, 3 to 4 hours or overnight.

8. Store in an airtight container in layers, with parchment or waxed paper between each layer, at room temperature for up to 5 days or in the freezer for up to 3 months.

CHOCOLATE-KISSED SNOWBALLS

Snowballs have long been a classic Christmas cookie—rich, buttery, shortbread hazelnut cookies rolled in icing sugar that simply melt in your mouth. And then in the 1970s, someone figured out you could stuff a chocolate kiss in the middle. Game. Over.

Makes 2 dozen cookies ❄ **Prep Time: 20 minutes** ❄ **Total Time: 30 minutes plus chilling**

1 cup icing sugar, divided

1 cup salted butter

1 tsp vanilla extract

⅔ cup finely chopped toasted nuts (such as hazelnuts or pecans, see tip)

2 cups flour

24 chocolate candy kisses, unwrapped

TIP:
To toast the nuts, place them on a small baking sheet and bake for 7 to 8 minutes in a 350°F oven. Lightly toss occasionally, until lightly browned on all sides. Remove and let cool completely before using or chopping.

1. Preheat the oven to 325°F. Line a baking sheet with parchment paper.

2. In a stand mixer with the paddle attachment or in a large bowl using a handheld mixer, beat ¼ cup of the icing sugar and the butter and vanilla on medium speed until smooth and creamy. Add the nuts and mix until thoroughly combined. Gradually add the flour and mix until combined.

3. Refrigerate the dough for 1 hour. The secret to snowballs is to use extremely hard dough, cold from the fridge.

4. Shape a heaping tablespoon of dough around a chocolate kiss, forming a 1-inch ball. Place on the prepared baking sheet 1 inch apart. Repeat until all the dough and kisses are used.

5. Bake for 9 to 10 minutes, then check the bottoms to see if they are browned. You want to dry these out, rather than cook them through. You do not want to overbake them! Once the bottoms are browned, remove from the oven and let rest for 1 minute.

6. Place the remaining ¾ cup icing sugar in a bowl. Roll the balls in icing sugar and return to the baking sheet. Once they have cooled and the sugar has set somewhat, roll each ball in icing sugar again and place on wire racks to cool completely.

7. Store in an airtight container in layers, with parchment or waxed paper between each layer, at room temperature for up to 5 days or in the freezer for up to 3 months.

Cherry Snowballs

Here's yet another version of the snowball cookie, this time with a cherry and coconut base! This is an easy one to make in bulk, so double the recipe if you'd like—you're already making a mess of the kitchen, getting coconut everywhere!

Makes 4 dozen cookies ✳ **Prep Time: 40 minutes** ✳ **Total Time: 2 hours plus chilling and setting**

SNOWBALLS

1½ cups salted butter, softened

¾ cup icing sugar

1 egg

2 Tbsp maraschino cherry juice

3 cups flour

1 cup quick-cooking rolled oats

½ cup finely chopped almonds

48 maraschino cherries, drained on paper towels

GLAZE

4 cups icing sugar

¼ cup maraschino cherry juice

8–10 Tbsp whipping cream or heavy cream

6 cups unsweetened finely shredded coconut

1. For the snowballs: In a stand mixer with the paddle attachment or in a large bowl using a handheld mixer, beat the butter and icing sugar on medium speed until smooth. Add the egg, beating well. Mix in the maraschino juice until combined. Stir in the flour, oats, and almonds until fully incorporated.

2. Cover the bowl with plastic wrap and refrigerate for 4 hours or overnight if wanted.

3. Preheat the oven to 325°F.

4. Flatten a tablespoon of dough into a circle. Place a cherry in the middle, then wrap the dough around the cherry, sealing it completely. Place the wrapped cherries on two ungreased baking sheets, spacing them 2 inches apart. (You will need to set some aside for further batches.)

5. Bake, one sheet at a time, for 18 to 20 minutes or until golden brown. Transfer the cookies to wire racks to cool completely.

6. For the glaze: In a large bowl, combine the icing sugar and maraschino juice. Add 8 tablespoons of cream, stirring until the consistency is thick enough for dipping. Add more cream if needed.

7. Place the coconut on a large plate. Line a large baking sheet with waxed paper.

8. Place a cookie flat on a fork (do not pierce) and dip it into the glaze, coating completely and letting the excess drip off. Place the cookie in the coconut and roll until completely covered, then transfer to the prepared baking sheet. Repeat with the remaining cookies. You might have to sprinkle some coconut over top to fill in any gaps. Set aside, uncovered, and let the glaze harden, about 1 hour.

9. Store in an airtight container in layers, with parchment or waxed paper between each layer, at room temperature for up to 5 days or in the freezer for up to 3 months.

CHAPTER TWO

GINGERBREAD & FESTIVELY FILLED COOKIES

There are some flavors that just shout "CHRISTMAS!" Gingerbread has to be one of them, right? And it can be used in so many ways, whether sandwiched with icing (page 70) or stamped with a cookie press (page 65) or, of course, cut into classic gingerbread people (page 66). Much like the sugar cookies in the previous chapter, this is a recipe for the whole family to come together over. Even now, at 17 and 19 years old, my own kids still messily make gingerbread people, stars, Christmas trees, and more with me. While there are no chipmunk cheeks full of cherries, cookies do somehow tend to disappear before they are decorated, especially when Mr. Kitchen Magpie joins us. Decorating gingerbread cookies with Royal Icing (page 250) has become a messy but fun tradition for us.

Jumping off from gingerbread, there are so many other festive flavors, nibs, and bits to fill your cookies with! Peppermint is another no-brainer, making the Peppermint Candy Chocolate Cookies (page 78) a tasty traditional treat, while the Fruitcake Cookies (page 74) are a new family favorite that I've taken to making year-round. They're like an amped-up hermit cookie, the best part being the crunchy pecans. My recipe is for a very big batch, so it's perfect for your cookie exchange!

For a bit more of a challenge, with all the reward, the Lace Cookies on page 93 are like those cookies you get at the big-box store, but more delicate. And biscotti (page 94), while simple in theory, does take a few more steps than Mincemeat Cookies (page 89).

Nothing beats a cookie jar full of cookies that you keep filling up throughout the holiday season for snacking. I hope that you find a new family favorite in this chapter!

Gingerbread Press Cookies

My grandma would make gingerbread press cookies for Christmas every year, taking the time and care to create perfect little shapes dusted with colored sugar. Cookie press cookies have fallen out of favor in the past decade or so, likely because they can be fiddly and time-consuming to make, but Christmas is the perfect time of year to make cookies simply for the joy of it, without being in a rush to hurry up and get them done. That said, you don't have to use a cookie press for this recipe: simply roll the dough into balls and press with fork tines to shape.

Makes 3–4 dozen cookies ❄ **Prep Time: 20 minutes** ❄ **Total Time: 1 hour plus chilling**

Cookie press with assorted shape plates (optional)

3 cups flour

2 tsp ground ginger

1½ tsp ground cinnamon

¼ tsp ground cloves

¼ tsp salt

⅛ tsp ground white pepper

¾ cup butter

¾ cup packed brown sugar

1 egg

¾ cup fancy molasses

1 tsp vanilla extract

Sanding sugar or colored sprinkles or nonpareils, for decorating

1. In a large bowl, whisk together the flour, ginger, cinnamon, cloves, salt, and pepper. Set aside.

2. In a stand mixer with the paddle attachment or in a large bowl using a handheld mixer, gently cream the butter and brown sugar on low speed until well combined, but be careful to stop before the mixture becomes light and fluffy. Mix in the egg, then the molasses and vanilla, until combined. With the mixer on low speed, gradually add the flour mixture, mixing until fully incorporated.

3. Transfer the dough to a large piece of plastic wrap and wrap tightly. Refrigerate for 15 to 20 minutes or until slightly chilled. As you press cookies in step 5, keep dough you're not currently working with in the fridge.

4. Meanwhile, preheat the oven to 375°F. Line two baking sheets with parchment paper.

5. If using a cookie press, fill the press with dough and stamp the shapes onto the prepared baking sheets, spacing them 2 inches apart. (If not using a press, roll the dough into ¾-inch balls, place 2 inches apart on the prepared baking sheets, and flatten slightly with a fork.) Sprinkle with your chosen decorations. (You will need to set some aside for further batches.)

6. Bake, one sheet at a time, for 8 to 9 minutes or until lightly browned around the edges. Be careful not to overbake! Immediately transfer the cookies to wire racks to cool completely.

7. Store in an airtight container in layers, with parchment or waxed paper between each layer, at room temperature for up to 5 days or in the freezer for up to 3 months.

GINGERBREAD CUT-OUT COOKIES

The deep, heavy spice flavor in this recipe comes from the molasses and is complemented by the sweet royal icing, so don't skip it! This is an ideal cookie exchange recipe: not only is it big-batch, but it's fun to receive cookies decorated by other people—especially if the kids are involved!

Makes 65–70 cookies ❄ **Prep Time: 1 hour** ❄ **Total Time: 2 hours, 20 minutes plus chilling**

6 cups flour (approx.)

2 Tbsp ground ginger

2 tsp ground cinnamon

½ tsp ground nutmeg

½ tsp ground allspice

1½ tsp baking soda

½ tsp salt

1 cup butter

1⅓ cups packed brown sugar

½ cup granulated sugar

2 eggs

1⅓ cups cooking molasses

1 tsp vanilla extract

Royal Icing (page 250)

Assorted candies and sprinkles

1. In a medium bowl, whisk together the flour, ginger, cinnamon, nutmeg, allspice, baking soda, and salt. Set aside.

2. In a stand mixer with the paddle attachment or in a large bowl using a handheld mixer, beat the butter, brown sugar, and granulated sugar on high speed until smooth and creamy, about 2 minutes. Add the eggs, one at a time, beating well after each. Mix in the molasses and vanilla on low speed until combined. With the mixer on low speed, gradually add the flour mixture, mixing until fully incorporated. If the dough is too sticky to roll out, add more flour, 1 tablespoon at a time, until you can roll it.

3. Divide the dough into 4 equal pieces and shape each into a disk. Wrap each disk with plastic wrap and refrigerate for at least 3 hours or for up to 3 days.

4. Preheat the oven to 350°F. Line two baking sheets with parchment paper. (Cookies will be baked in batches.)

5. On a lightly floured work surface, roll out each disk to ¼-inch thickness, rotating after each roll to prevent sticking. Use more flour as needed to prevent stickiness. Using a cookie cutter, and rerolling the scraps as needed, cut out 65 to 70 cookies. Place on the prepared baking sheets, spacing them 2 inches apart.

6. Bake, one sheet at a time, for 10 to 11 minutes or until just browned, the edges are set, and the dough looks dull and is firm. Let cool for 5 minutes, then transfer to wire racks to cool completely.

7. Decorate the cookies with the royal icing, candies, and sprinkles. Let set for 3 to 4 hours or overnight.

8. Store in an airtight container in layers, with parchment or waxed paper between each layer, at room temperature for up to 7 days or in the freezer for up to 3 months.

Gingersnap Cookies

Crispy on the outside and chewy on the inside, these are my family's traditional ginger cookies! This recipe yields a softer cookie, which I prefer to a crunchier one. But if you want them to live up to the "snap" in the name, omit the egg yolk and bake them for a little longer, until the cookies are lightly browned on the bottom and set in the middle.

Makes 6–7 dozen cookies ❄ **Prep Time: 20 minutes** ❄ **Total Time: 1 hour, 25 minutes plus chilling**

2½ cups flour

1 Tbsp ground ginger

1 tsp ground cinnamon

¼ tsp ground allspice

¼ tsp ground cloves

2 tsp baking soda

½ teaspoon salt

1 cup butter, softened

1¼ cups granulated sugar, divided

½ cup packed brown sugar

1 egg

1 egg yolk (optional)

⅓ cup cooking molasses

1 tsp vanilla extract

1. In a medium bowl, whisk together the flour, ginger, cinnamon, allspice, cloves, baking soda, and salt. Set aside.

2. In a stand mixer with the paddle attachment or in a large bowl using a handheld mixer, beat the butter, ¾ cup of the granulated sugar, and the brown sugar on high speed until smooth and creamy, about 2 minutes. Add the egg and egg yolk (if using, for a softer cookie), one at a time, beating well after each. Mix in the molasses and vanilla until combined. With the mixer on low speed, gradually add the flour mixture, mixing until fully incorporated.

3. Cover the bowl tightly with plastic wrap and refrigerate for at least 2 hours or for up to 3 days.

4. Preheat the oven to 350°F. Line two baking sheets with parchment paper.

5. Place the remaining ½ cup granulated sugar in a bowl. Roll the dough into 1-inch balls, then roll in the sugar to coat. Place on the prepared baking sheets, spacing them 2 inches apart. (You will need to set some aside for further batches.)

6. Bake, one sheet at a time, for 8 to 9 minutes or until the tops have cracked all over and the edges look set. (For crunchier cookies, continue to bake for another 3 to 4 minutes or until the middle looks set as well.) Let cool completely on the baking sheets.

7. Store in an airtight container in layers, with parchment or waxed paper between each layer, at room temperature for up to 5 days or in the freezer for up to 3 months.

GINGER CREAM COOKIES

These soft, cakey ginger cookies are sandwiched with cream cheese frosting to create the perfect sweet treat. Roll the frosted edge in sprinkles, for the kids, or a little bit of candied ginger for the adult crowd.

Makes 2 dozen sandwich cookies ❄ Prep Time: 20 minutes ❄ Total Time: 1 hour, 10 minutes

3½ cups flour

1 Tbsp ground ginger

1 tsp ground nutmeg

¼ tsp ground cloves

2 tsp baking soda

½ tsp salt

½ cup boiling water

1 tsp white vinegar

½ cup butter

½ cup granulated sugar

1 egg yolk

1 cup fancy molasses

1 cup Cream Cheese Frosting (page 249)

Sprinkles or candied ginger (optional)

1. Preheat the oven to 350°F. Line two large baking sheets with parchment paper.

2. In a medium bowl, whisk together the flour, ginger, nutmeg, cloves, baking soda, and salt. Set aside.

3. In a heatproof glass measuring cup, combine the boiling water and vinegar. Set aside.

4. In a stand mixer with the paddle attachment or in a large bowl using a handheld mixer, beat the butter and sugar on high speed until smooth and creamy, about 2 minutes. Add the egg yolk, beating well. Mix in the molasses on low speed until combined. With the mixer on medium speed, gradually add the flour mixture and vinegar mixture, alternating between the two, until both are fully incorporated. Beat the dough for another minute.

5. Using a tablespoon-sized cookie scoop, scoop dough balls onto the prepared baking sheets, spacing them about 2 inches apart. (You will need to set some aside for further batches.)

6. Bake, one sheet at a time, for 10 to 12 minutes or until the edges are set and the middle has cooked. Let cool completely on the baking sheets.

7. Place a scoop of frosting on the flat side of one cookie, then sandwich with another cookie, flat side down. Repeat with the remaining cookies and frosting. If desired, roll the edges in sprinkles or candied ginger.

8. Store in an airtight container in layers, with parchment or waxed paper between each layer, in the fridge for up to 5 days or in the freezer for up to 3 months.

Russian Teacakes

These cookies are known by so many different names, it's hard to list them all—Russian teacakes, pecan sandies, wedding cookies, snowball cookies, hazelnut meltaways, and more! The name changes by region and the kinds of nuts used. The key to these crumbly cookies is chopping the nuts very finely so that, when you bite into the cookie, it melts in your mouth.

Makes 3 dozen cookies ❄ **Prep Time: 20 minutes** ❄ **Total Time: 1 hour, 20 minutes plus chilling**

2 cups sifted flour

½ tsp salt

1 cup butter

⅓ cup + 1½ cups icing sugar, divided

1½ tsp vanilla extract (for pecan sandies or Russian teacakes), or ¼ tsp almond extract (for wedding cookies)

1¼ cups finely chopped pecans (for pecan sandies), hazelnuts (for Russian teacakes), or almonds (for wedding cookies)

1. In a medium bowl, whisk together the flour and salt. Set aside.

2. In a stand mixer with the paddle attachment or in a large bowl using a handheld mixer, beat the butter and ⅓ cup of the icing sugar on medium speed until smooth. Mix in the vanilla until combined. Gradually mix in the flour mixture on low speed until smooth. Stir in the nuts until evenly distributed.

3. Cover the bowl with plastic wrap and refrigerate for at least 4 hours or until the dough is firm.

4. Preheat the oven to 325°F.

5. Shape the dough into walnut-sized balls (for pecan sandies or Russian teacakes) or crescents (for wedding cookies). Place on ungreased baking sheets, spacing them 2 inches apart. (You will need to set some aside for a third batch.)

6. Bake, one sheet at a time, for 18 to 20 minutes or until golden. Transfer the cookies to wire racks to cool completely.

7. Place the remaining 1½ cups icing sugar in a bowl. Roll the cookies in sugar to coat.

8. Store in an airtight container in layers, with parchment or waxed paper between each layer, at room temperature for up to 5 days or in the freezer for up to 3 months.

FRUITCAKE COOKIES

These old-fashioned fruitcake cookies are our family's new favorite Christmas cookie. They're similar to a hermit cookie, but contain mostly fruit, with only a little bit of cookie dough. Soaking the raisins in amaretto liqueur really takes these to the next level! If you prefer not to use amaretto, apple or orange juice works too. This is a very-big-batch recipe (when my sister tested it, she sarcastically wrote "yield = 30 million cookies"), but that just makes it perfect for cookie exchanges or for keeping your cookie jar filled the entire holiday season!

Makes 8 dozen cookies ❄ **Prep Time: 20 minutes** ❄ **Total Time: 2 hours plus chilling**

1 cup golden raisins

1 cup Thompson raisins

¼ cup amaretto liqueur, apple juice, or orange juice

2¾ cups flour

1 tsp ground cinnamon

½ tsp ground nutmeg

¼ tsp ground cloves

1 tsp baking soda

1 tsp salt

1 cup butter, softened

1 cup packed brown sugar

¼ cup cooking molasses

3 eggs

4 cups chopped pecans

2 cups chopped pitted dates

1 container (8 oz/227 g) diced candied pineapple

1 container (16 oz/454 g) whole red and green glace cherries, chopped

1. Place the golden and Thompson raisins in a liquid measuring cup. Pour in the amaretto and stir. Let soak for at least 2 hours or overnight (the longer, the better).

2. Preheat the oven to 350°F. Line two baking sheets with parchment paper.

3. In a medium bowl, whisk together the flour, cinnamon, nutmeg, cloves, baking soda, and salt. Set aside.

4. In a stand mixer with the paddle attachment or in a large bowl using a handheld mixer, beat the butter and brown sugar on high speed until smooth and creamy, about 2 minutes. Mix in the molasses until combined. Add the eggs, one at a time, beating well after each. With the mixer on low speed, gradually add the flour mixture, mixing until fully incorporated. Using a wooden spoon, stir in the raisin mixture, pecans, dates, pineapple, and cherries until evenly distributed.

5. Drop the dough by tablespoonfuls onto the prepared baking sheets, spacing them 2 inches apart. (You will need to set some dough aside for further batches.)

6. Bake, one sheet at a time, for 10 to 12 minutes or until the edges are set and browned. Let cool on the baking sheet for 5 minutes, then transfer the cookies to wire racks to cool completely.

7. Store in an airtight container in layers, with parchment or waxed paper between each layer, at room temperature for up to 5 days or in the freezer for up to 3 months.

Peanut Butter Candy Cookies

For this famous "blossom" Christmas cookie, I use my favorite peanut butter cookie recipe as the base, then top with whatever candy I'm feeling in the moment! These cookies are so easy to customize with anything from chocolate kisses to mini peanut butter cups—my personal preference for the ultimate peanut butter cookies! Santa-shaped milk chocolates also make fun cookies for kids and adults alike. Natural peanut butter can have too much oil in it, so I tend to stick with traditional sugar-loaded peanut butter here and for all of my holiday baking.

Makes 3 dozen cookies ❄ **Prep Time: 25 minutes** ❄ **Total Time: 55 minutes**

1¼ cups flour

½ tsp baking powder

½ tsp baking soda

½ tsp salt

½ cup butter, softened

1 cup packed brown sugar

1 egg

½ cup smooth peanut butter (not natural)

2 tsp vanilla extract

½ cup granulated sugar or red or green sanding sugar

36 chocolate candies of choice, unwrapped (I like Christmas-shaped ones, mini peanut butter cups, or Hershey's Kisses)

1. Preheat the oven to 375°F. Line two large baking sheets with parchment paper.

2. In a medium bowl, whisk together the flour, baking powder, baking soda, and salt. Set aside.

3. In a stand mixer with the paddle attachment or in a large bowl using a handheld mixer, beat the butter and brown sugar on medium speed until smooth and creamy, about 2 minutes. Add the egg, beating well. Mix in the peanut butter and vanilla on low speed until combined. With the mixer on low speed, gradually add the flour mixture, beating constantly until a soft dough forms.

4. Pour the granulated sugar onto a small plate. Roll the dough into 1-inch balls, then roll in the sugar to coat completely. Place on the prepared baking sheets, spacing them 2 inches apart. (You will need to set some aside for a third batch.)

5. Bake, one sheet at a time, for 8 to 10 minutes or until the edges are golden brown and set. Immediately press a chocolate candy into the center of each cookie. Let cool completely on the baking sheets.

6. Store in an airtight container in layers, with parchment or waxed paper between each layer, at room temperature for up to 5 days or in the freezer for up to 3 months.

PEPPERMINT CANDY CHOCOLATE COOKIES

When it comes to the chocolate topping for these cookies, it's choose-your-own-adventure! I prefer a minty white chocolate, but you can use whatever says "Christmas" most to you! One of my favorite parts of Christmas is all the different festive chocolates and treats that companies release only for the holidays, so it's the perfect time to experiment with your baking!

Makes 3 dozen cookies ❄ Prep Time: 20 minutes ❄ Total Time: 50 minutes

2½ cups flour

¾ cup unsweetened cocoa powder

1 tsp baking soda

½ tsp salt

1 cup butter

1 cup packed brown sugar

1½ cups granulated sugar, divided

2 eggs

1 tsp vanilla extract

36 peppermint white chocolates, unwrapped

1. Preheat the oven to 350°F. Line two baking sheets with parchment paper.

2. In a medium bowl, whisk together the flour, cocoa, baking soda, and salt. Set aside.

3. In a stand mixer with the paddle attachment or in a large bowl using a handheld mixer, beat the butter, brown sugar, and 1 cup of the granulated sugar on high speed until smooth and creamy, about 2 minutes. Add the eggs, beating well after each addition. Mix in the vanilla until combined. With the mixer on low speed, gradually add the flour mixture, mixing until fully incorporated.

4. Pour the remaining ½ cup granulated sugar onto a small plate. Roll the dough into 1-inch balls, then roll in the sugar to coat completely. Place on the prepared baking sheets, spacing them about 1½ inches apart. (You will need to set some aside for a third batch.)

5. Bake, one sheet at a time, for 8 to 10 minutes or until the edges are set. Immediately press a peppermint chocolate into the center of each cookie. Let cool completely on the baking sheets.

6. Store in an airtight container in layers, with parchment or waxed paper between each layer, at room temperature for up to 5 days or in the freezer for up to 3 months.

Fruity White Chocolate Macadamia Nut Cookies

These cookies are a must-bake treat year-round, but when you add dried cranberries or cherries, they become a tangy new Christmas classic. Classic cookie or festive flavor—the choice is yours!

Makes 4 dozen cookies ❄ **Prep Time: 20 minutes** ❄ **Total Time: 1 hour, 10 minutes**

2¼ cups flour

1 tsp baking soda

½ tsp salt

¾ cup butter, softened

1 cup packed brown sugar

½ cup granulated sugar

2 eggs

2 tsp vanilla extract

1 cup white chocolate chips

1 cup coarsely chopped macadamia nuts

1 cup coarsely chopped sweetened dried cranberries or cherries

1. Preheat the oven to 350°F. Line two large baking sheets with parchment paper.

2. In a medium bowl, whisk together the flour, baking soda, and salt. Set aside.

3. In a stand mixer with the paddle attachment or in a large bowl using a handheld mixer, beat the butter, brown sugar, and granulated sugar on high speed until smooth and creamy, about 2 minutes. Add the eggs, one at a time, beating well after each. Mix in the vanilla until combined. With the mixer on low speed, gradually add the flour mixture, mixing until fully incorporated. Using a wooden spoon, stir in the chocolate chips, macadamia nuts, and cranberries until evenly distributed.

4. Drop the dough by rounded tablespoons onto the prepared baking sheets, spacing them 2 inches apart. (You will need to set some aside for further batches.)

5. Bake, one sheet at a time, for 10 to 12 minutes or until the edges are golden brown and the middles are almost baked through but not completely set. Let cool completely on the baking sheets.

6. Store in an airtight container in layers, with parchment or waxed paper between each layer, at room temperature for up to 5 days or in the freezer for up to 3 months.

CRANBERRY ORANGE COOKIES

Cranberry-orange is the classic wintertime flavor pairing for baked goods—why should cookies be any exception? These cakey cookies are bursting with bright orange flavor and tangy cranberries—and when topped with a citrus icing or glaze? Perfection.

Makes 4 dozen cookies ❄ **Prep Time: 20 minutes** ❄ **Total Time: 1 hour**

2½ cups flour

1 tsp baking powder

½ tsp baking soda

½ tsp salt

1 cup butter

1 cup granulated sugar

1 Tbsp orange zest

1 egg

1 tsp orange extract

2 cups sweetened dried cranberries

½ cup Citrus Icing or Glaze (page 249), made with orange zest and juice, thick for icing or thin for glaze, as desired

1. Preheat the oven to 350°F. Line two baking sheets with parchment paper.

2. In a medium bowl, whisk together the flour, baking powder, baking soda, and salt. Set aside.

3. In a stand mixer with the paddle attachment or in a large bowl using a handheld mixer, beat the butter and sugar on medium speed until light and fluffy. Beat in the orange zest. Add the egg, beating well. Mix in the orange extract on low speed until combined. With the mixer on low speed, gradually add the flour mixture, mixing until fully incorporated and the dough comes together nicely. Using a wooden spoon, stir in the cranberries until evenly distributed.

4. Using a tablespoon-sized cookie scoop, scoop dough balls onto the prepared baking sheets, spacing them 2 inches apart. (You will need to set some dough aside for further batches.)

5. Bake, one sheet at a time, for 10 minutes or until the edges are very lightly browned and the middles are set. Do NOT let these overbrown! Let cool completely on the baking sheets, then transfer the cookies to wire racks.

6. Drizzle the icing or glaze over the cookies and let set.

7. Store in an airtight container in layers, with parchment or waxed paper between each layer, at room temperature for up to 5 days or in the freezer for up to 3 months. Put a piece of bread in the container with the cookies to keep them from drying out. Do not refrigerate, or they will go rock hard.

Chewy Spiced Date Cookies

We sure love our date desserts here on the Prairies! I had to include the quintessential Date Squares (page 197), but I also wanted to share these chewy, spicy date-based cookies. Cloves and nutmeg bring holiday pizzazz and that oh-so-familiar Christmas baking aroma. These cookies might seem familiar: if you replace half the dates with raisins, you have hermit cookies!

Makes 4 dozen cookies ❄ **Prep Time: 20 minutes** ❄ **Total Time: 1 hour, 20 minutes plus chilling**

3 cups flour

2 tsp ground cinnamon

½ tsp ground cloves

½ tsp ground nutmeg

1 tsp baking soda

½ tsp salt

1 cup butter, softened

½ cup granulated sugar

½ cup packed brown sugar

3 eggs

1 tsp vanilla extract

2 cups finely chopped dates

1 cup finely chopped walnuts

1. In a large bowl, whisk together the flour, cinnamon, cloves, nutmeg, baking soda, and salt. Set aside.

2. In a stand mixer with the paddle attachment or in a large bowl using a handheld mixer, beat the butter, granulated sugar, and brown sugar until light and fluffy. Add the eggs, one at a time, beating well after each. Mix in the vanilla until combined. Gradually add the flour mixture, mixing until fully incorporated. Using a wooden spoon, stir in the dates until evenly distributed.

3. Cover the bowl with plastic wrap and refrigerate for 2 hours or until the dough is firm.

4. Preheat the oven to 350°F. Line two baking sheets with parchment paper.

5. Pour the walnuts onto a plate. Roll the dough into 1-inch balls, then roll in the walnuts to coat completely. Place on the prepared baking sheets, spacing them 2 inches apart. (You will need to set some aside for further batches.)

6. Bake, one sheet at a time, for 12 to 14 minutes or until the edges are firm and the tops are just set (you don't want to overbake, or they will be dry). Let cool on the baking sheet for 5 minutes, then transfer the cookies to wire racks to cool completely.

7. Store in an airtight container in layers, with parchment or waxed paper between each layer, at room temperature for up to 5 days or in the freezer for up to 3 months.

BROWN BUTTER
CHOCOLATE CHIP COOKIES

Christmas is the time of year when we love to dabble in different baking methods—when we take the time to slow down and enjoy our baking a little bit more. If you haven't tried them yet, brown butter chocolate chip cookies should be on your to-dabble list! By cooking the milk proteins in the butter, you get a nutty, toasted toffee flavor that can't be beat. To get all nerdy, this is because of the Maillard reaction, which is the chemical process that creates those flavor compounds in the butter. It's a technique that is well worth mastering!

Makes 4 dozen cookies ❄ Prep Time: 20 minutes ❄ Total Time: 1 hour

¾ cup butter

2¼ cups flour

1 tsp baking soda

½ tsp salt

1 cup packed brown sugar

½ cup granulated sugar

2 eggs

2 tsp vanilla extract

2 cups semisweet chocolate chips

2–3 tsp sea salt flakes

1. Preheat the oven to 350°F. Line two large baking sheets with parchment paper.

2. Get the bowl for your stand mixer or a large bowl ready beside you—you'll need to move fast in the next step!

3. Place the butter in a small saucepan and heat over medium heat, stirring and swirling. Once it starts to foam, it will quickly turn golden brown. As soon as this happens, remove it from the heat and pour it into the bowl to stop the cooking process. Let the butter cool down, but it doesn't have to solidify: simply let it cool to lukewarm.

4. Meanwhile, in a medium bowl, whisk together the flour, baking soda, and salt. Set aside.

5. In a stand mixer with the paddle attachment or in a large bowl using a handheld mixer, beat the still-liquid butter, brown sugar, and granulated sugar on high speed until smooth and creamy, about 2 minutes. Add the eggs, one at a time, beating well after each. Mix in the vanilla on low speed until combined. With the mixer on low speed, gradually add the flour mixture, mixing until fully incorporated. Using a wooden spoon, stir in the chocolate chips until evenly distributed.

6. Using a tablespoon-sized cookie scoop, scoop dough balls onto the prepared baking sheets, spacing them 2 inches apart. (You

will need to set some dough aside for further batches.) Sprinkle with 2 teaspoons of the sea salt, adding more as needed to taste.

7. Bake, one sheet at a time, for 10 to 12 minutes or until the edges are golden brown and set but the centers are still slightly under-done. Let cool on the baking sheet for 5 minutes, then transfer the cookies to wire racks to cool completely.

8. Store in an airtight container in layers, with parchment or waxed paper between each layer, at room temperature for up to 5 days or in the freezer for up to 3 months.

Mincemeat Cookies

Another one for the mincemeat-loving crowd! In fact, these seasonal treats are so good, you might even convince the mincemeat haters with this one. For the easiest cookies ever, you can buy a jar of commercially prepared mincemeat.

Makes 3 dozen cookies ⁕ **Prep Time: 20 minutes** ⁕ **Total Time: 40 minutes**

3¼ cups flour

1 tsp baking soda

1 tsp ground cinnamon

½ tsp ground cloves

½ tsp ground allspice

½ tsp salt

1 cup butter

¾ cup granulated sugar

¾ cup packed brown sugar

2 eggs

2 cups mincemeat

2 tsp vanilla extract

1. Preheat the oven to 400°F. Line two baking sheets with parchment paper.

2. In a large bowl, whisk together the flour, baking soda, cinnamon, cloves, allspice, and salt. Set aside.

3. In a stand mixer with the paddle attachment or in a large bowl using a handheld mixer, beat the butter, granulated sugar, and brown sugar on high speed until smooth and creamy, about 2 minutes. Add the eggs, one at a time, beating well after each. Mix in the mincemeat and vanilla on low speed until combined. With the mixer on low speed, gradually add the flour mixture, mixing until fully incorporated.

4. Using a tablespoon-sized cookie scoop, scoop dough balls onto the prepared baking sheets, spacing them 2 inches apart. (You will need to set some dough aside for a third batch.)

5. Bake, one sheet at a time, for 8 to 10 minutes or until the edges are set and the tops are lightly browned. Let cool on the baking sheet for 5 minutes, then transfer the cookies to wire racks to cool completely.

6. Store in an airtight container in layers, with parchment or waxed paper between each layer, at room temperature for up to 5 days or in the freezer for up to 3 months.

PUMPKIN RAISIN NUT COOKIES

Pumpkin isn't only for autumn—every Christmas cookie platter should feature lovely, spicy, pumpkin-flavored cookies. You can replace the raisins with chocolate chips, if desired. These are soft, cakey cookies that store extremely well, which is another reason they make for a great cookie exchange choice: not only are they easy to make, but you can surprise everyone with pumpkin cookies in December! Make sure to use canned plain pumpkin, not pumpkin pie filling: the filling is spiced and sugared, and here we're making our own flavors.

Makes 3 dozen cookies ❊ **Prep Time: 20 minutes** ❊ **Total Time: 1 hour**

2¼ cups flour

2 tsp baking powder

1 tsp baking soda

½ tsp salt

2 tsp ground cinnamon

½ tsp ground nutmeg

¼ tsp ground ginger

½ cup butter

½ cup granulated sugar

½ cup packed brown sugar

2 eggs

1 cup canned pumpkin (not pumpkin pie filling)

1 tsp vanilla extract

1 cup raisins or chocolate chips

1 cup chopped pecans or walnuts

1. Preheat the oven to 350°F. Line two large baking sheets with parchment paper.

2. In a medium bowl, whisk together the flour, baking powder, baking soda, salt, cinnamon, nutmeg, and ginger. Set aside.

3. In a stand mixer with the paddle attachment or in a large bowl using a handheld mixer, beat the butter, granulated sugar, and brown sugar on high speed until smooth and creamy, about 2 minutes. Add the eggs, one at a time, beating well after each. Mix in the pumpkin and vanilla on low speed until combined. With the mixer on low speed, gradually add the flour mixture, mixing until fully incorporated. Using a wooden spoon, stir in the raisins and nuts until evenly distributed.

4. Using a tablespoon-sized cookie scoop, scoop dough balls onto the prepared baking sheets, spacing them 2 inches apart. (You will need to set some dough aside for a third batch.) Flatten the balls slightly with the back of the scoop.

5. Bake, one sheet at a time, for 12 to 13 minutes or until the edges are set and the tops are lightly browned. (These cookies do not flatten when baked.) Let cool on the baking sheet for 5 minutes, then transfer the cookies to wire racks to cool completely.

6. Store in an airtight container in layers, with parchment or waxed paper between each layer, at room temperature for up to 5 days or in the freezer for up to 3 months.

Lace Cookies

Lace cookies are my favorite treat from Costco, the store I can never seem to leave without trying all the samples and spending more money than I intended—especially at Christmastime! The recipe name itself indicates how delicate (like lace!) these are, so a light hand and care is needed to make them. They are the perfect gift when you want to spend some time mastering a new cookie!

Makes 3 dozen sandwich cookies ❄ **Prep Time: 50 minutes** ❄ **Total Time: 1 hour, 35 minutes**

1 cup almond meal (see tip)

½ cup flour

½ cup + 1 Tbsp salted butter, divided

½ cup granulated sugar

½ cup packed brown sugar

2 Tbsp dark corn syrup

2 Tbsp liquid honey

2 tsp vanilla extract

1 cup semisweet or milk chocolate chips

TIP:

To make fresh almond meal, grind 2 cups of whole raw almonds to a coarse ground meal in a food processor or even a blender. You should get 1 cup of almond meal once done!

1. In a small bowl, whisk together the almond meal and flour.

2. In a medium saucepan, combine ½ cup of the butter, granulated sugar, brown sugar, corn syrup, and honey over medium heat. Bring to a boil, stirring the entire time.

3. Remove from the heat and stir in the vanilla until combined. Stir in the almond meal mixture until just combined. Let cool and thicken for 10 minutes, stirring once halfway through.

4. Meanwhile, preheat the oven to 350°F. Line two large baking sheets with parchment paper.

5. Using a teaspoon-sized cookie scoop, drop scant spoonfuls of dough onto the prepared baking sheets, spacing them at least 3 inches apart. (You will need to set some aside for further batches.)

6. Bake, one sheet at a time, for 4 to 7 minutes or until evenly golden brown all over. Watch closely! Different ovens will give varying baking times. Let cool on the baking sheet for 5 minutes or until they firm up, then carefully transfer the cookies to wire racks to cool completely.

7. Place the chocolate chips and remaining 1 tablespoon of the butter in a large microwave-safe glass measuring cup. Microwave on medium power in 20-second increments, stirring after each, until the chocolate chips have almost completely melted (a few lumps are okay). Stir until fully melted and smooth.

8. Dollop chocolate onto a cookie, then gently top with another. Repeat with the remaining cookies and chocolate, then let cool completely.

9. Store in an airtight container in layers, with parchment or waxed paper between each layer, at room temperature for up to 3 days, in the fridge for up to 1 week, or in the freezer for up to 3 months.

CHRISTMAS BISCOTTI

These make a wonderful gift, as biscotti stores well when made ahead, is pretty and festive when speckled with candied fruit, and packages up like a charm for gifting. The key to making biscotti is to let it completely dry out—this is why it stores so well. They're lovely to dip into your Christmas morning coffee while watching the kids tearing into gifts, and are perfect with hot chocolate on a quiet Christmas night, after the festivities, while you ignore the mess you have to clean up on Boxing Day.

Makes 4–5 dozen cookies ❄ **Prep Time: 30 minutes** ❄ **Total Time: 2 hours, 10 minutes plus chilling**

5½ cups flour

1 Tbsp baking powder

½ tsp salt

½ cup butter

2 cups granulated sugar

6 eggs

1½ tsp almond extract

1½ cups mixed diced candied fruit (red and green cherries are my favorite)

2 cups white chocolate melting wafers

1. In a large bowl, whisk together the flour, baking powder, and salt. Set aside.

2. In a stand mixer with the paddle attachment or in a large bowl using a handheld mixer, beat the butter and sugar on medium speed until smooth and creamy, about 2 minutes. Add the eggs, one at a time, beating well after each. Mix in the almond extract on low speed until combined. With the mixer on low speed, gradually add the flour mixture, mixing constantly until well combined. Using a wooden spoon, stir in the candied fruit until evenly distributed.

3. Cover the bowl with plastic wrap and refrigerate for 1 hour.

4. Preheat the oven to 325°F. Line two large baking sheets with parchment paper.

5. Cut the chilled dough into 4 equal pieces. Shape each piece into a 12-inch-long rounded log and place lengthwise on a prepared baking sheet. You should be able to fit 2 logs on each sheet.

6. Bake, one sheet at a time, for 25 to 30 minutes or until lightly browned. Remove from the oven, leaving the oven on, and let cool on the baking sheet for 5 minutes.

7. Once the loaves are cool enough to handle, transfer them to a cutting board and cut into 1-inch-thick slices. Return the slices to the baking sheets, arranging them cut side up in a single layer.

8. Bake, one sheet at a time, for 15 to 20 minutes, flipping them once halfway through, until dried out and lightly browned on each side. Let cool completely on a wire rack.

9. Melt the chocolate wafers according to the package directions. Dip the top of each biscotti into the melted chocolate, then return to the baking sheets. Let set until the chocolate hardens.

10. Store in an airtight container in layers, with parchment or waxed paper between each layer, at room temperature for up to 5 days or in the freezer for up to 3 months.

Chocolate Meringue Corn Cereal Cookies

These light-as-air, crunchy cookies are an old family favorite of ours, and are always a hit at every cookie exchange! This recipe doubles perfectly for a larger batch, if desired. It is also a popular gluten-free choice when I need to make something that fits the bill; just double-check all your ingredients (like the corn cereal and icing sugar) to make sure they are gluten-free, and you have a great gluten-free cookie in your baking repertoire when you need one.

Makes 2 dozen cookies ⁖ **Prep Time: 20 minutes** ⁖ **Total Time: 1 hour, 20 minutes**

1 cup sifted icing sugar

¼ tsp salt

2 egg whites

2 cups unsweetened cornflakes cereal

1 cup sweetened flaked coconut

1 cup mini semisweet chocolate chips

½ tsp vanilla extract

24 glace cherry halves or chocolate candy kisses

Christmas sprinkles (optional)

1. Preheat the oven to 300°F. Line two baking sheets with parchment paper.

2. In a small bowl, whisk together the icing sugar and salt. Set aside.

3. In a stand mixer with the whisk attachment or in a large bowl using a handheld mixer, beat the egg whites until stiff. With the mixer on medium speed, gradually add the sugar mixture, beating constantly until satiny and smooth. Using a wooden spoon, gently stir in the cereal, coconut, chocolate chips, and vanilla until evenly distributed.

4. Using a teaspoon-sized cookie scoop, scoop dough balls onto the prepared baking sheets, spacing them 2 inches apart. Press a cherry half or kiss into the center of each ball, and cover with a few Christmas sprinkles (if using).

5. Bake, one sheet at a time, for 25 to 30 minutes or until the cookies are light like meringue and completely dried out.

6. Store in an airtight container in layers, with parchment or waxed paper between each layer, at room temperature for up to 5 days or in the freezer for up to 3 months.

CHAPTER THREE

CANDIES

Candy making is notoriously difficult.

I want to kick off with that statement so that you're prepared. I had a lot of recipe testers helping with this cookbook, and the recipes they found the most challenging were for candy. Of course, some factors affecting candy making are beyond your control, such as the precise room temperature and the humidity in your house.

But each of my recipes has been tested over and over so it can be made successfully! Make sure to follow any tips I offer for a recipe, follow the temperatures as stated, and allow yourself time. You simply cannot be in a rush when making candy.

It's all worth it for this chapter of true candy recipes—meaning you use a thermometer to accurately measure the temperature. For example, the kinds of fudge in this chapter (pages 116 to 120) have to be cooked to exact temperatures, like the Divinity Candy on page 116; my other fudges can be found in the following chapter of confections!

There's nothing more satisfying than making a batch of Homemade Caramels (page 115), in your own kitchen or mastering something that feels completely impossible like Peanut Brittle (page 104), and it can be done with practice and some tricks of the trade that I will get into. Making your own candy at home is also an excellent way to save money on sweet treats, since fudge, pralines, brittles, and good quality caramel corn can be very expensive to buy in stores.

You'll be a candy-making machine in no time. And while you're getting the hang of it, there'll never be a tastier trial period.

Candy Tips ✳ ✳ ✳ ✳ ✳ ✳ ✳

HOW TO ACCURATELY MEASURE TEMPERATURE

I have fully switched to using an instant-read thermometer, which I've found much more reliable than a clip-on candy thermometer. (The bonus of an instant-read is that you can clean it off and use it for meats or anything else you cook. My instant-read thermometer is the single most used item in my kitchen.) While testing the candy mixture, I swirl the thermometer tip through four or five different spots to get the most accurate reading. When you start doing this, you'll see that the temperature can vary by 2 to 3 degrees within little pockets of the mixture. Once most of the spots are the same temperature I recommend in the recipe, carry on.

EMBRACE CORN SYRUP

A big moment for me: for the first time in my life, I have mastered brown sugar fudge, aka Penuche (page 120)! I've been trying for years! The secret is to add corn syrup. Corn syrup is an invert sugar, which inhibits the formation of sugar crystals in candy. It also gives your candies a smooth texture, which is especially noticeable in the fudge and also helps when making pralines (page 108). So when you see me call for corn syrup, know that it's for a scientific reason!

PRACTICE

I know, no one wants to hear that. But I tried three different versions of the Pineapple Fudge on page 119 before I finally came up with a recipe that actually works! I ruined about 15 batches of brown sugar fudge before figuring out the aforementioned corn syrup secret. Eat your mistakes—crumbly fudge is still fudge—figure out your mistakes, then try again!

Nutty Caramel Popcorn

This is a copycat recipe for that beloved tinned caramel popcorn that is always gifted around the holiday season. Loaded with caramel, pecans, and almonds, this treat is so easy to make yourself. And aren't the best gifts those that are homemade?

Makes 16 cups ❄ Prep Time: 40 minutes ❄ Total Time: 1 hour, 40 minutes

12 cups popped popcorn, unpopped kernels removed

2 cups toasted whole almonds (see tip, page 59)

2 cups toasted pecan, halved

2 cups packed brown sugar

1 cup salted butter

½ cup dark corn syrup

½ tsp baking soda

1 tsp vanilla extract

1. Preheat the oven to 250°F. Line a large rimmed baking sheet (also known as a jelly roll pan) with parchment paper.

2. Place the popcorn, almonds, and pecans in an exceptionally large heatproof bowl.

3. In a medium saucepan, bring the brown sugar, butter, and corn syrup to a rolling boil over high heat. Reduce the heat to medium-high and bring the mixture to the soft-crack stage (270°F to 290°F on an instant-read thermometer) without stirring.

4. Remove from the heat and stir in the baking soda and vanilla.

5. Pour the caramel mixture over the popcorn and nuts, and stir until completely coated.

6. Scoop out onto the baking sheet, arranging in an even layer.

7. Bake for 1 hour, stirring every 15 minutes. Let cool completely, then break apart into your desired size of clusters.

8. Store in an airtight container at room temperature for up to 5 days or in the freezer for up to 3 months.

PEANUT BRITTLE

This recipe reminds me of the gold-wrapped butterscotch candies found in every grandma's candy dish. The creamy butterscotch shatters perfectly and, with salted peanuts, makes for fabulous peanut brittle!

Makes 2 dozen pieces ❄ **Prep Time: 5 minutes** ❄ **Total Time: 30 minutes plus cooling**

2½ cups granulated sugar

1 cup butter

½ cup light corn syrup

½ cup water

¼ tsp salt

2½ cups salted dry-roasted peanuts

1 tsp baking soda

1. Line a large rimmed baking sheet (also known as a jelly roll pan) with parchment paper.

2. In a large saucepan, combine the sugar, butter, corn syrup, water, and salt. Cook over medium-high heat, stirring occasionally, until the caramel reaches 250°F on an instant-read thermometer. Add the peanuts and cook until the caramel reaches 300°F.

3. Remove from the heat and carefully stir in the baking soda. The mixture will bubble.

4. Immediately scrape the brittle onto the prepared baking sheet, spreading it into a thin, even layer. Let cool completely, about 60 minutes, then break into pieces.

5. Store in an airtight container in layers, with parchment or waxed paper between each layer, at room temperature for up to 2 weeks or in the freezer for up to 3 months.

English Toffee

This is a big-batch recipe for my English toffee, perfect for holiday gifting. A version with a smaller yield can be found in my first cookbook, but for Christmas baking everything needs to be oversized, right? So I tested it out as a double batch using my oversized rimmed baking sheet that is 20 × 14 inches, and it fits perfectly. If you don't have a baking sheet that large, you can divide the toffee between two smaller sheets.

Makes 40–45 pieces ❄ Prep Time: 5 minutes ❄ Total Time: 25 minutes plus chilling

2⅔ cups granulated sugar

2 cups salted butter

½ cup water

2 Tbsp light corn syrup

2 tsp vanilla extract

3 cups milk chocolate chips

2 cups toasted chopped or slivered almonds

1. Line a 20- × 14-inch rimmed baking sheet, or 2 smaller rimmed baking sheets, with parchment paper.

2. In a large, heavy-bottomed saucepan, combine the sugar, butter, water, and corn syrup. Cook over medium heat, stirring constantly, to the hard-crack stage (295°F to 300°F on an instant-read thermometer).

3. Remove from the heat and quickly stir in the vanilla.

4. Spread the mixture on the prepared baking sheet(s) in an even layer of about ¼-inch thickness. While the toffee is still hot, sprinkle the chocolate chips over top in an even layer. Once the chips have melted (they turn shiny when ready), use a spatula to spread out the chocolate evenly.

5. Sprinkle with the almonds and press lightly into an even layer on the chocolate to ensure they stick. Refrigerate until set, about 20 to 25 minutes.

6. Using your hands, break the toffee into pieces.

7. Store in an airtight container in layers, with parchment or waxed paper between each layer, at room temperature for up to 5 days or in the freezer for up to 3 months.

PEANUT PRALINES

While very finicky, this Southern treat can be mastered with some practice (although don't try it on a humid day!). First, always use a thermometer, as there is no visual cue when it's ready; it's all about the temperature read. When it comes to stirring the finished product, stir only until it's just thick enough to hold its shape but hasn't set in the pan yet, then work quickly to dole it out onto the sheets. As soon as you stop stirring, it will start to set. The result should be smooth, not grainy. Don't worry if there are white spots after the pralines set—that's simply crystallization: the sugar is trying to revert to its original form. Pecans are traditional, but peanuts are my favorite for praline—and peanuts are much cheaper for when you are first practicing!

Makes 2 dozen pralines ❄ **Prep Time: 20 minutes** ❄ **Total Time: 30 minutes plus setting**

1 cup granulated sugar

1 cup packed brown sugar

⅔ cup whipping cream or heavy cream

¼ cup salted butter

2 tsp light corn syrup

2 cups dry-roasted peanuts or toasted pecan halves (see tip, page 59)

2 tsp vanilla extract

1. Line two baking sheets with parchment paper.

2. In a medium, heavy-bottomed saucepan, combine the granulated sugar, brown sugar, cream, butter, and corn syrup. Bring to a boil over medium heat, then boil, stirring constantly, until the mixture reaches 238°F on an instant-read thermometer.

3. Remove from the heat and stir in the peanuts and vanilla. Keep stirring slowly until the mixture thickens slightly and starts to hold its shape, about 2 to 3 minutes.

4. Working quickly, before it sets, drop heaping tablespoons of the mixture onto the prepared baking sheets, spacing them 1½ inches apart. Let cool and harden at room temperature for 45 minutes.

5. Store in an airtight container in layers, with parchment or waxed paper between each layer, at room temperature for up to 1 week or in the freezer for up to 3 months.

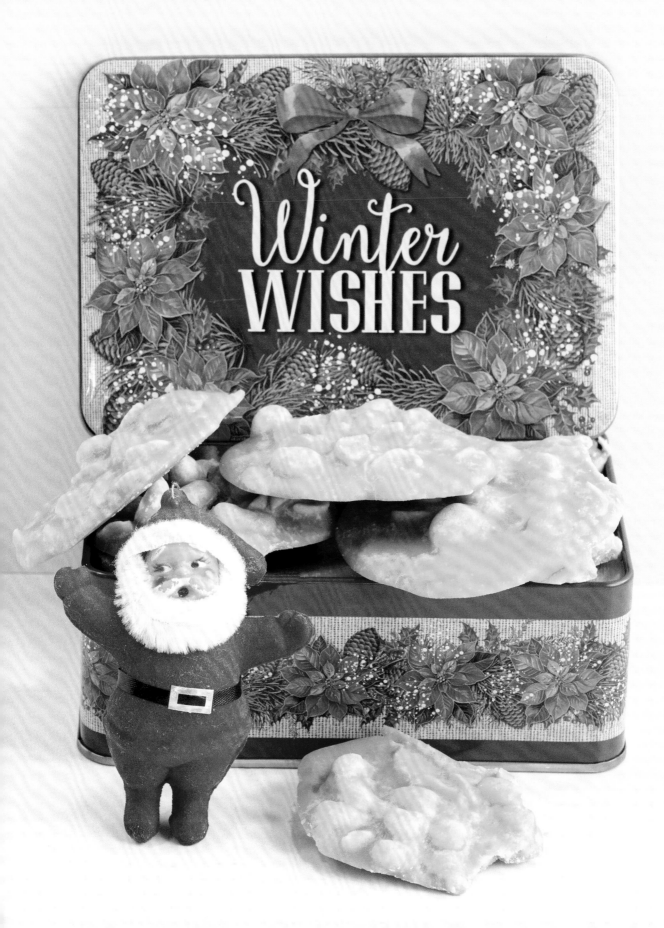

Maple Walnut Pralines

A delicious Canadian twist on a Southern classic. This version of the praline was taste-tested by my entire extended family over Christmas, to a unanimous verdict: we prefer it to the classic! Maybe it's because we Canadians really do love our maple syrup, but it's most likely the fact that this version simply blows the traditional one out of the water, flavor-wise. It reminds me of the little candied bites you find in a good maple walnut ice cream. As with the Peanut Pralines (page 108), you'll need to work quickly when spooning the pralines to set.

Makes 2 dozen pralines ❄ **Prep Time: 20 minutes** ❄ **Total Time: 30 minutes plus setting**

2 cups packed brown sugar

1 cup maple syrup

1 cup whipping cream or heavy cream

¼ cup salted butter

2 tsp light corn syrup

1½ cups halved toasted walnut (see tip, page 59)

⅛ tsp ground cinnamon

1. Line two baking sheets with parchment paper.

2. In a medium, heavy-bottomed saucepan, combine the brown sugar, maple syrup, cream, butter, and corn syrup. Bring to a boil over medium heat, then boil, stirring constantly, until the mixture reaches 238°F on an instant-read thermometer.

3. Remove from the heat and stir in the walnuts and cinnamon until evenly distributed. Keep stirring slowly until the mixture thickens slightly and starts to hold its shape, about 2 to 3 minutes.

4. Working quickly, before it sets, drop heaping tablespoons of the mixture onto the prepared baking sheets, spacing them 1½ inches apart. Let cool and harden at room temperature for 45 minutes.

5. Store in an airtight container in layers, with parchment or waxed paper between each layer, at room temperature for up to 1 week or in the freezer for up to 3 months.

MOLASSES TAFFY

This old-fashioned taffy is for molasses lovers! Make sure you have helping hands to pull the taffy—make an afternoon of it with the family. As with all candies, you'll need patience and lots of time—as taffy must be pulled for anywhere from 10 to 20 minutes before it's done!

Makes 90–100 pieces ❄ **Prep Time: 10 minutes** ❄ **Total Time: 40 minutes plus pulling plus wrapping**

1½ cups cooking molasses

¾ cup granulated sugar

¾ cup packed brown sugar

½ cup water

1½ tsp white vinegar

5–6 Tbsp butter, divided

½ tsp baking soda

¼ tsp salt

TIP:

Taffy is best made on a non-humid day, and with a 4- to 5-quart pot (this is especially important in step 3).

1. Butter a large rimmed baking sheet (also known as a jelly roll pan) with butter.

2. In a 4- to 5-quart, heavy-bottomed saucepan, combine the molasses, granulated sugar, brown sugar, water, and vinegar. Heat over medium-low heat, stirring constantly until the sugar is dissolved. Continue cooking, stirring frequently and occasionally using a pastry brush dipped in hot water to remove any sugar crystals that form on the sides of the pan, until the mixture reaches 250°F on an instant-read thermometer.

3. Add 3 tablespoons of the butter and the baking soda and salt. The mixture should foam up. Keep stirring until the foaming subsides, about 3 to 4 minutes.

4. Pour the mixture onto the prepared pan and let cool for 5 minutes.

5. Butter a large metal spatula (the solid, flat type you flip burgers with is best) and use it to lift the edge of the candy, folding the candy over itself, like folding a pancake in half. The candy will pool out again, so continue to move and fold it to keep it from stiffening, until it is cool enough to pick up.

6. Once the candy is cool enough to handle, divide it into 2 to 4 equal pieces, depending on how many assistants you have (you need two people per piece). Grease your hands with butter. Pull the taffy out in short lengths, twisting it as you go. Keep stretching until it is golden and becomes very hard to pull. This may take between 10 and 20 minutes, depending on how big the taffy piece is.

7. Pull each taffy piece into one final rope, 1 inch in diameter.

8. Carefully butter the blades of a pair of scissors, then cut the rope into bite-sized pieces. Wrap each piece in parchment or waxed paper.

9. Store in an airtight container at room temperature for up to 1 week or in the freezer for up to 3 months. Make sure to thaw at room temperature until completely softened before eating, or you'll break a tooth!

Homemade Caramels

Although they're time-consuming to make, nothing beats homemade caramels for the holiday season! Just put on a Christmas movie and keep stirring. By the time the city girl with a stressful corporate job realizes her soulmate is her first love from the small town she grew up in, you'll have melt-in-your-mouth, chewy, buttery caramels well worth the time!

Makes about 115 pieces ❄ Prep Time: 10 minutes ❄
Total Time: 1 hour, 15 minutes plus setting plus wrapping

1½ cups granulated sugar

1½ cups packed brown sugar

2 cups whipping cream or heavy cream

1 cup light corn syrup

1 cup salted butter, cut into small chunks

2 tsp vanilla extract

Sea salt flakes, for topping (optional)

1. Line a 13- × 9-inch pan with parchment paper. (Tip: Place the bottle of vanilla and a teaspoon measuring spoon in the pan—that way, you won't forget to add the vanilla at the end. It works, trust me!)

2. In a 6-quart, heavy-bottomed saucepan, combine the granulated sugar, brown sugar, cream, corn syrup, and butter. Heat over medium-low heat, stirring constantly, until everything has melted. Cook, stirring gently and constantly, until the mixture reaches 244°F on an instant-read thermometer. This can take 1 hour or longer! You can also test it by dropping a small portion of the mixture into a bowl of cold water; if it forms a firm ball, it's ready.

3. Remove from the heat and stir in the vanilla. (See? You can't pour it into the pan without moving the vanilla bottle first!)

4. Pour the caramel into the prepared pan. Tap the pan gently on the counter a few times to release any air bubbles. Sprinkle with sea salt (if using). Let firm up at room temperature for 3 to 4 hours.

5. Meanwhile, cut waxed paper into about 115 small pieces for wrapping the caramels.

6. Slice the caramel into 1-inch squares, for a total of about 115 caramels, and individually wrap them in waxed paper.

7. Store in an airtight container at room temperature for up to 1 month, or freeze in the container or in heavy-duty freezer bags for up to 6 months.

DIVINITY CANDY

When I asked my mom which candy she remembers most from her childhood, this was it. That said, it's "practice makes perfect" when it comes to these! Make sure to set aside some uninterrupted time on a day that is not humid—for this and all candy recipes, a minute's distraction can mean all the difference between success and failure. But for Mom, it's all worth it.

Makes 2 dozen pieces ❄ Prep Time: 25 minutes ❄ Total Time: 30 minutes plus setting

Stand mixer with the whisk attachment

2 egg whites

⅛ tsp salt

2½ cups granulated sugar

⅔ cup water

½ cup light corn syrup

1 tsp vanilla extract

1 cup chopped cherries or chopped toasted walnuts (see tip, page 59)

TIP:
If you overbeat your candy to the point where it seizes up and becomes grainy, beat in hot water, 1 tablespoon at a time, until the mixture comes together again.

1. In the stand mixer, whip the egg whites and salt on medium speed until light and fluffy. Set aside.

2. Line a large baking sheet with parchment paper.

3. In a saucepan, combine the sugar, water, and corn syrup. Bring to a boil over medium-high heat, then boil, stirring frequently, until the mixture reaches 260°F on an instant-read thermometer. Remove from the heat.

4. Replace the whisk with the paddle. With the mixer on medium speed, beat the egg whites quickly to fluff them up again if needed. In a slow, continuous small stream, drizzle the hot candy mixture into the egg whites, beating continuously. Beat on high speed for 6 to 7 minutes or until the candy is no longer shiny. Depending on humidity, the time it takes to beat the candy until done can vary. Test by placing a small spoonful on the prepared baking sheet. When the candy keeps its shape and doesn't pool into a puddle, it's ready (see tip). Stir in the vanilla and cherries until evenly distributed.

5. Drop by tablespoonfuls onto the prepared baking sheet. Let stand overnight to dry out.

6. Store in an airtight container in layers, with parchment or waxed paper between each layer, at room temperature for up to 1 week or in the freezer for up to 3 months.

Pineapple Fudge

This is a lovely tropical twist on standard fudge. Pineapple extract isn't easy to find anymore, so to get this to taste like your grandma's pineapple fudge, you must source a food-grade pineapple-flavored oil (I use LorAnn Oils, which you can find online or at some bulk food stores). It's worth the hunt for Christmas baking, trust me! This is a very sweet fudge; adding nuts helps cut the sweetness, but feel free to try it with and without for comparison. It just means more taste-testing—which is never unwelcome!

Makes 2 dozen pieces ❄ Prep Time: 20 minutes ❄ Total Time: 40 minutes plus chilling

3 cups granulated sugar

1 can (19 oz/540 mL) crushed pineapple, well drained

½ cup whipping cream or heavy cream

1 Tbsp light corn syrup

2 Tbsp salted butter

½ tsp pineapple-flavored baking oil

1 cup chopped toasted nuts (optional)

1–2 drops yellow food coloring (optional)

1. Line an 8-inch square pan with parchment paper, leaving enough overhang at either end to use as handles.

2. In a large, heavy-bottomed saucepan, combine the sugar, pineapple, cream, and corn syrup. Bring to a boil over medium-high heat, then boil, stirring occasionally, until the mixture reaches 236°F on an instant-read thermometer.

3. Remove from the heat and place the butter on top of the mixture, but do not stir it in. Let cool to 125°F.

4. Stir in the melting butter, pineapple oil, nuts, and enough food coloring (if using) to reach your desired color.

5. Beat with a wooden spoon until the fudge turns creamy colored instead of clear, and starts to lose its shine, then turn out into the prepared pan. Refrigerate until set, about 2 hours.

6. Lift the slab out of the pan using the parchment handles. Slice into squares.

7. Store in an airtight container in layers, with parchment or waxed paper between each layer, at room temperature for up to 5 days or in the freezer for up to 3 months.

PENUCHE

Brown sugar fudge, or penuche, is infamous for seizing up and becoming crumbly if you even look at it the wrong way. Don't make this on a humid or hot day. If you have a cool, dry day, heat the fudge to the proper temperature and let it cool to room temperature before beating, you stand a good chance of success with this recipe!

Makes 2 dozen pieces ❄ **Prep Time: 20 minutes** ❄ **Total Time: 35 minutes plus chilling**

3 cups packed brown sugar

1 cup half-and-half cream

2 Tbsp corn syrup

1½ Tbsp salted butter

1½ tsp vanilla extract

1. Line an 8-inch square pan with parchment paper, leaving enough overhang at either end to use as handles.

2. Pour the brown sugar, cream, and corn syrup into a heavy-bottomed saucepan that you can use a handheld mixer in; it should be stainless steel, with no coating. Heat over low heat, stirring until the sugar is dissolved and the mixture comes to a low, rolling boil. Stirring occasionally, bring it to 236°F on an instant-read thermometer.

3. Remove from the heat and place the butter on top of the mixture, but do not stir it in. Let cool in the pot for 10 minutes.

4. Add the vanilla and, using a handheld mixer, beat for 2 to 3 minutes or until creamy. Pour into the prepared pan and refrigerate until chilled, about 60 minutes.

5. Lift the slab out of the pan using the parchment handles. Slice into squares.

6. Store in an airtight container in layers, with parchment or waxed paper between each layer, at room temperature for up to 5 days or in the freezer for up to 3 months.

Sponge Candy

This is one of my favorite treats; it's perfect whether plain or dipped in chocolate. Like the Divinity Candy on page 116, this recipe simply won't work if it's humid or hot: you need a cool, dry day, which luckily we get plenty of during our Canadian winters! If you are a lover of sponge candy, it's worth the time and effort to master this recipe, as it's one of the most expensive treats to buy for what is basically chocolate-covered sugar, and it freezes like a dream, for snacking on later!

Makes 20–24 pieces ✳ Prep Time: 30 minutes ✳ Total Time: 1 hour plus chilling

¾ cup packed brown sugar

¼ cup granulated sugar

1 cup light corn syrup

2 tsp baking soda, sifted

12 oz milk or dark baking chocolate, coarsely chopped (optional)

1. Line a 9-inch square pan with parchment paper. Grease the parchment lightly with cooking spray.

2. In a very large, very-heavy-bottomed saucepan, combine the brown sugar, granulated sugar, and corn syrup. The mixture will expand, so make sure your pot can accommodate this! Bring the mixture to a boil, stirring continuously, then boil, stirring, until the candy reaches 292°F on an instant-read thermometer.

3. Remove from the heat and quickly sprinkle the baking soda over top. Stir quickly to thoroughly mix the baking soda throughout the candy. The candy will start to expand and bubble.

4. Pour the candy into the prepared pan in an even layer, starting at one end and pouring to the other end without using a spoon and without touching the mixture. You can't touch it in any way, or the mixture will lose its bubbles and height. Let cool completely at room temperature about 60 minutes, then break into pieces by hand.

5. If dipping in chocolate, line a large baking sheet with parchment or waxed paper. Place the chocolate in a microwave-safe glass measuring cup and microwave on medium power in 20-second increments, stirring after each, until melted and smooth.

6. Take a piece of candy and shake or brush off any crumbs, then dip one side or end into the melted chocolate. Let the excess chocolate drip off, then place on the prepared baking sheet. Repeat with the remaining candy. Refrigerate until the chocolate is set, about 30 minutes.

7. Store in an airtight container in layers, with parchment or waxed paper between each layer, at room temperature for up to 1 week or in the freezer for up to 2 months.

CHAPTER FOUR

CONFECTIONS

Confections are those perfect little bites of sweet bliss that we all love to bake and indulge in during the holiday season. One of the joys of writing this cookbook has been rediscovering old recipes that I haven't made in decades and had completely forgotten about. (Even though I love to bake, I can't possibly make every single recipe in this book every year—I am only human!) If I had to choose one that sums up the holiday season and all my memories of it, it would be the Peanut Butterscotch Cereal Clusters on page 160, which I hadn't had in decades! But rest assured, it's back on my must-make list.

Some of the confections in this chapter are time-consuming to make, but they are all relatively easy. My sister now makes the Homemade Peppermint Patties (page 144) year-round and keeps them in the freezer to snack on. The Chocolate-Covered Cherries on page 128 also take some time, but it's well worth it in the end, especially since you can make a boozy adult version that you can't buy in stores! That fact right there sums up why you should definitely try making them at home! My dad always has a not-so-secret stash of his Coconut Caramel Corn Cereal Treats (page 163) in the freezer year-round, but we leave his stash alone and just ask him to make fresh ones to share for Christmas.

As well, you'll find in this chapter a lot of no-bake treats, which I adore. The best recipes, when it comes to the busy holiday season, are those where you simply melt and then mix the ingredients together. The proof is in the (Christmas) pudding! Of the 20 recipes here, only 4 require you to turn on the oven, and even those recipes are as easy as can be.

Many of these treats are fast and easy, and will save your sanity during the busy holiday season!

Moose Chow

Here on the Canadian Prairies, this classic no-bake cereal treat is less "puppy chow" and definitely more "moose chow." In Canada, we don't get all the Chex cereals, so we have to use what we have in our stores, and in my opinion, the Crispix corn and rice cereal makes this classic sweet munching mix even tastier.

Makes 11–12 cups ❅ **Prep Time: 20 minutes** ❅ **Total Time: 20 minutes**

1 bag (10 oz/300 g) semisweet chocolate chips

⅔ cup smooth peanut butter (not natural)

¼ cup salted butter

1 tsp vanilla extract

1 box (12 oz/350 g) Crispix or Chex corn and rice cereal

3 cups icing sugar, divided

1 cup red and green candy-coated chocolates (such as M&M's)

1. Line a large baking sheet with parchment paper.

2. In a large microwave-safe bowl, combine the chocolate chips, peanut butter, and butter. Microwave on medium power in 20-second increments, stirring after each, until the chocolate chips have almost completely melted (a few lumps are okay). Stir until fully melted, combined, and smooth. Stir in the vanilla.

3. Place the cereal in a large bowl. Pour the melted chocolate mixture over top and gently stir to combine.

4. Pour 1 cup of the icing sugar into each of two zip-top bags. Divide the cereal between the two bags. Add another ½ cup icing sugar on top of the cereal in each bag. Seal, then shake each bag, making sure all the pieces are coated in sugar. You can also add the candy-coated chocolates and shake again for extra sweetness.

5. Turn out the candy pieces onto the prepared baking sheet and let cool completely.

6. Store in an airtight container at room temperature for up to 5 days or in the freezer for up to 3 months.

CHOCOLATE-COVERED CHERRIES

This is one of those no-bake goodies that is so easy to make in the comfort of your own kitchen, you'll wonder why you've ever bothered running to the store for it. (I mean it: I truly never buy fudge anymore.) For a decadent adult treat, first soak the drained cherries in your preferred liquor for 24 hours. You can enjoy the resulting cherry-flavored liqueur in a cocktail, like our Manhattan on page 271, and use the alcohol-soaked cherries in this recipe. The boozy version is the perfect Christmas gift, because it can't be bought in stores!

Makes 3 dozen cherries ❄ **Prep Time: 1 hour plus soaking** ❄ **Total Time: 1 hour plus chilling and soaking**

36 maraschino cherries with stems, well drained, reserving 2 Tbsp juice

¾ cup brandy, amaretto, or whisky (optional)

3–4 cups sifted icing sugar

¼ cup salted butter, softened

1 bag (10 oz/300 g) dark chocolate chips

1. If soaking the cherries, place them in a bowl with your preferred liquor and let soak for 24 hours. Drain and save the liqueur for cocktails. Pat the cherries dry with paper towels, then place them on paper towels to dry to absorb extra moisture.

2. Line a large baking sheet with parchment or waxed paper.

3. In a medium bowl, mix 3 cups of the icing sugar with the butter and the reserved cherry juice until a heavy, soft dough forms. You might need more icing sugar depending on a number of factors, like the humidity in your house or the type of butter used or how well they sift. The dough should be slightly tacky, but should not stick to your hands. Form into a disk and tightly wrap with plastic wrap, then refrigerate the dough for 30 minutes.

4. Form 1 tablespoon of dough into a flat circle about 1 inch in diameter. Place a cherry in the center, then wrap the dough around it, enclosing it completely. Place on the prepared baking sheet. Repeat with the remaining cherries. Refrigerate for 30 minutes.

5. Place the chocolate chips in the top of a double boiler or a large bowl set on top of a pot of water, making sure the bottom does not touch the water. Bring the water to a rolling boil over medium-high heat and stir the chocolate until melted, combined, and smooth.

6. Holding a cherry by its stem, quickly dip it into the melted chocolate. Let any excess chocolate drip off, then return the cherry to the baking sheet. Repeat with the remaining cherries. Return the sheet to the fridge to set the chocolate, about 10 to 15 minutes.

7. Store in an airtight container in layers, with parchment or waxed paper between each layer, in the fridge for 1 week before serving (this lets the cherries get juicy). The cherries will keep in the fridge for up to another 2 weeks or in the freezer for up to 3 months.

Peanut Butter Fudge

I'm not too proud of a baker to admit that fudge often likes to seize up on me. And I'll be vulnerable with you: peanut butter fudge is one of the worst. This is the only recipe I've found to be as foolproof as fudge can possibly get! You don't have to cook it to a certain temperature, and by using the marshmallow fluff, you get a soft, non-grainy peanut butter fudge that is easy to make.

Makes 2 dozen pieces ❄ **Prep Time: 5 minutes** ❄ **Total Time: 30 minutes plus chilling**

2½ cups granulated sugar

⅔ cup evaporated milk

1½ cups smooth peanut butter (not natural)

1 jar (7 oz/198 g) marshmallow fluff

1 tsp vanilla extract

1. Line a 9-inch square pan with parchment paper, then lightly butter the paper.

2. In a large, heavy-bottomed saucepan, heat the sugar and milk to a low, rolling boil. Boil for 3 minutes, stirring continuously.

3. Remove from the heat and stir in the peanut butter, marshmallow fluff, and vanilla.

4. Pour into the prepared pan and, using a spatula, spread in an even layer. Refrigerate for 2 hours, then cut into 24 squares.

5. Store in an airtight container in layers, with parchment or waxed paper between each layer, at room temperature for up to 5 days or in the freezer for up to 3 months.

EASY CHOCOLATE FUDGE

I've been making this fudge for almost 20 years! It's made in the microwave and is so easy to customize to your liking with different extract flavors and add-ins to give it your personal flair. In fact, it's SO easy, I used to make them as Christmas gifts for the kids' teachers, because you can line up prepared pans and make many different kinds of fudge in under an hour.

Makes 2 dozen pieces ❄ **Prep Time: 20 minutes** ❄ **Total Time: 20 minutes plus chilling**

1 can (14 oz or 300 mL) sweetened condensed milk

9½ oz semisweet baking chocolate, coarsely chopped

1½ tsp vanilla extract

1 cup mix-ins of choice, divided (I like chopped walnuts, mini peanut butter cups, or Christmas-colored hard-shell chocolates)

1. Line an 8-inch square pan with parchment paper.

2. In a large microwave-safe glass measuring cup, combine the condensed milk and chocolate. Microwave on medium power for 1 minute. Stir, then microwave for 45 seconds. Stir until the chocolate is completely melted. Stir in the vanilla until combined. Let cool until just warm, then stir in ¾ cup of your mix-ins of choice.

3. Pour the fudge into the prepared pan. Sprinkle the remaining ¼ cup of mix-ins over top, then gently press down into the top of the fudge. Refrigerate for a few hours, until cooled completely. Slice into 24 squares.

4. Store in an airtight container in layers, with parchment or waxed paper between each layer, at room temperature for up to 5 days or in the freezer for up to 3 months.

Gumdrop Frosting Fudge

Do you eat frosting straight from the can? Do you consider cake the vehicle to get frosting into your mouth? Then this recipe is for you! Using a can of premade frosting, this classic "cheater" no-bake recipe tastes like frosting (of course), it's loaded with festive gumdrops, and only needs three ingredients—perfect for making with the kids! It's also completely mix-and-match-able: try different combinations of frosting, chocolate chips, and mix-ins.

Makes 2 dozen pieces ❄ **Prep Time: 20 minutes** ❄ **Total Time: 20 minutes plus chilling**

1 can (16 oz/450 g) French vanilla frosting

1 bag (10 oz/300 g) white chocolate chips

1½ cups red and green jujubes, cut into large pieces

1. Line an 8-inch square pan with parchment paper.

2. Remove the lid and any foil covering from the icing so you are left with only a plastic container. Microwave the canned icing on high power for about 1 minute or until melted into a liquid.

3. Place the chocolate chips in a large microwave-safe bowl. Microwave on medium power in 20-second increments, stirring after each, until the chocolate chips have almost completely melted (a few lumps are okay). Stir until fully melted, combined, and smooth.

4. Quickly stir the warm icing into the melted chocolate (do this before either sets, or they won't combine properly). Stir in the jujubes until evenly distributed.

5. Pour the fudge into the prepared pan and refrigerate until firm. Slice into 24 squares.

6. Store in an airtight container in layers, with parchment or waxed paper between each layer, at room temperature for up to 5 days or in the freezer for up to 3 months.

CHOCOLATE NUT CLUSTERS

While we Johnstons love the rich flavor of cashews for these Christmas clusters, you can easily sub in your own favorite nut. Although it's trendy to make these in the slow cooker, I find the chocolate can burn and stick to the bottom of the pot. It's easier to heat it on the stovetop, watching it carefully to make sure the end result is perfect! Double this recipe and make it for gifts—it's so easy to prepare, but the cashews make it an always-welcome rich and decadent sweet treat!

Makes 3–4 dozen pieces ❄ **Prep Time: 20 minutes** ❄ **Total Time: 20 minutes plus chilling**

16 oz white baking chocolate, chopped

16 oz semisweet baking chocolate, chopped

4 cups salted cashews

¾ cup toffee bits

Sea salt flakes, for sprinkling (optional)

1. Line a large baking sheet with parchment or waxed paper.

2. Place the white and semisweet chocolates in a large, heavy-bottomed saucepan. Heat over low heat, stirring continuously, until melted and well combined.

3. Remove from the heat and stir in the cashews and toffee bits until well coated.

4. Drop by tablespoonfuls onto the prepared baking sheet. If using sea salt, sprinkle a few flakes on top of each before the melted chocolate sets. Refrigerate until completely set.

5. Store in an airtight container in layers, with parchment or waxed paper between each layer, at room temperature or in the fridge for up to 5 days or in the freezer for up to 3 months. I prefer my chocolate cold from the fridge when it's in candies like this. The fridge won't hurt them!

Christmas Coconut Macaroons

Make your chocolate coconut macaroons more festive with glace cherries and white chocolate! Or, if you prefer the classic recipe, see the tip. Since white chocolate is notorious for seizing at the slightest provocation, I prefer to use chocolate melting wafers to ensure baking success.

Makes 3–4 dozen macaroons ❄ **Prep Time: 25 minutes** ❄ **Total Time: 1 hour, 15 minutes plus setting**

4 cups sweetened shredded coconut

½ cup flour

½ tsp salt

1 can (14 oz or 300 mL) sweetened condensed milk

½ tsp almond extract

1 cup coarsely chopped red and green glace cherries

2 cups white chocolate melting wafers

TIP:
For standard macaroons, add 1 teaspoon vanilla with the almond extract, omit the cherries, and replace the white chocolate with semisweet.

1. Preheat the oven to 350°F. Line two baking sheets with parchment paper.

2. In a large bowl, combine the coconut, flour, and salt.

3. In a large liquid measuring cup, mix together the condensed milk and almond extract. Pour into the coconut mixture, stirring until well combined and the coconut is evenly coated. Stir in the cherries until evenly distributed.

4. Drop the batter by large tablespoonfuls onto the prepared baking sheets, spacing them 2 inches apart. (You will need to set some batter aside for further batches.)

5. Bake, one sheet at a time, for 10 to 12 minutes or until the tops and bottoms are toasted and browned. Let cool slightly on the baking sheet, until they are a safe temperature to touch.

6. Melt the chocolate wafers according to the package instructions. Dip the top of each macaroon in the chocolate, then return to the baking sheets. Let the chocolate harden completely and the macaroons cool completely.

7. Store in an airtight container in layers, with parchment or waxed paper between each layer, at room temperature for up to 5 days or in the freezer for up to 3 months.

MERINGUE CHRISTMAS TREE POPS

Swiss meringue is the best type of meringue when it comes to piping shapes and is almost always successful, even when the humidity in your house is relatively high. It can be piped into regular meringue shapes as well, but the trees are an easy treat for the kids!

Makes: 30 tree pops ❊ **Prep Time: 25 minutes** ❊ **Total Time: 2 hours, 25 minutes plus cooling**

Stand mixer with the whisk attachment

30 lollipop sticks (from the craft store)

3 egg whites

¾ cup granulated sugar

¼ tsp mint extract (banana, almond, or coconut are also delicious)

A few drops of green food coloring (optional)

Christmas nonpareils or sprinkles

1. Preheat the oven to 200°F. Line two baking sheets with parchment paper.

2. Place the egg whites and sugar in the heatproof metal bowl of the mixer.

3. In a large pot, bring 2 inches of water to a low simmer. Place the heatproof bowl over the pot, making sure the bottom does not touch the water, and heat the egg mixture, whisking constantly, until the sugar is dissolved. The mixture just needs to be warm to the touch. Watch out: do NOT cook the whites!

4. Secure the bowl to the mixer and whip on high speed until very stiff peaks form, 8 to 9 minutes. Add the flavoring and enough food coloring (if using) to reach your desired color, and beat until well combined.

5. Spoon the meringue into an icing bag fitted with a large round tip (or a disposable icing bag with the tip cut off). Pipe 30 small tree shapes onto the prepared baking sheets, leaving a few inches between each. Decorate with the nonpareils. Place a lollipop stick in the bottom of each tree to turn it into a pop.

6. Bake, one sheet at a time, for 60 minutes or until the pops are crisp and sound hollow when tapped. Let cool completely on the baking sheets.

7. Store in an airtight container in layers, with parchment or waxed paper between each layer, at room temperature for up to 5 days or in the freezer for up to 3 months.

BAKING TIP:
Pipe the shapes quickly, starting with the tree base, before the meringue hardens. If necessary, rewhip the meringue for another 1 to 2 minutes to soften.

Saltine Toffee Bark

Sweet, salty, and so easy to make—it's no wonder this treat is one of the most popular confections at Christmas. What is it about combining salty crackers with chocolate or caramel that says "holiday season"? I'm not sure, but we all seem to dip savory crackers into sweet things and call them desserts when it comes to Christmas, and as a sweet/salty combo lover, I am here for it every year!

Makes 36 squares ❄ **Prep Time: 20 minutes** ❄ **Total Time: 20 minutes plus chilling**

36 saltine crackers

1 cup packed brown sugar

1 cup butter

1 tsp vanilla extract

2 cups semisweet chocolate chips

Sprinkles or chopped nuts (optional)

1. Preheat the oven to 400°F. Line a rimmed baking sheet (also known as a jelly roll pan) with parchment paper.

2. Align the crackers side by side in a single layer on the prepared pan. Set aside.

3. In a small saucepan, combine the brown sugar and butter. Bring to a boil over medium heat, stirring frequently. Once the mixture reaches a boil, stop stirring and let boil for 3 minutes.

4. Remove from the heat and stir in the vanilla. Immediately—and carefully—pour the mixture over the crackers in an even layer. Use the back of a spoon to spread it out evenly.

5. Bake for 5 to 6 minutes or until the toffee mixture is bubbly. Sprinkle the chocolate chips over top. Let stand for 5 minutes to melt the chocolate, then use the back of a spoon to spread the chocolate into a smooth layer. Scatter the sprinkles or nuts over top (if using).

6. Refrigerate for 20 minutes or until the chocolate has set. Break into squares.

7. Store in an airtight container in layers, with parchment or waxed paper between each layer, at room temperature for up to 5 days or in the freezer for up to 3 months.

HOMEMADE PEPPERMINT PATTIES

Although they're a little fiddly to make, nothing beats homemade peppermint patties when it comes to Christmastime treat-making (bonus: no baking needed)!

Makes 6 dozen patties ❄ Prep Time: 30 minutes ❄ Total Time: 30 minutes plus chilling

1-inch round cookie cutter

¼ cup light corn syrup

¼ cup evaporated milk

4 Tbsp salted butter, softened, divided

1 tsp peppermint extract

5–6 cups sifted icing sugar, plus extra for sprinkling (see tip)

16 oz semisweet baking chocolate, coarsely chopped

Crushed candy canes or Christmas sprinkles, for topping (optional)

BAKING TIP:
The amount of icing sugar required will vary depending on the humidity, the butter used . . . those kinds of things. Simply add enough to get a stiff dough that can be rolled out after chilling.

1. In a stand mixer with the paddle attachment or in a large bowl using a handheld mixer, beat the corn syrup, milk, 2 tablespoons of the butter, and the peppermint extract on low speed until combined. With the mixer on low speed, add the icing sugar, 1 cup at a time, adding just enough to form a stiff dough.

2. Divide the dough in half and shape each into a disk. Wrap each disk tightly with plastic wrap and refrigerate for 20 minutes.

3. Line two large baking sheets with parchment or waxed paper.

4. Sprinkle icing sugar onto your work surface. Unwrap 1 disk and place on the work surface (keeping the second disk in the fridge). Sprinkle icing sugar over top, then roll out the dough to ¼-inch thickness. Using the cookie cutter, cut into circles. Place on a prepared baking sheet. Repeat with the remaining dough. Place the baking sheets in the freezer for 1 hour.

5. Place the chocolate and the remaining 2 tablespoons butter in a large microwave-safe glass measuring cup. Microwave in 20-second increments, stirring after each, until the chocolate has almost completely melted (a few lumps are okay). Stir until fully melted, combined, and smooth.

6. Place each frozen patty flat on a fork (do not pierce) and dip into the melted chocolate, coating completely. Let the excess drip off, then return to the baking sheet. Work quickly before the dough dissolves! Immediately sprinkle with crushed candy canes or sprinkles (if using). Repeat with the patties on the second sheet. Refrigerate for 20 minutes or until the chocolate has set.

7. Store in an airtight container in layers, with parchment or waxed paper between each layer, in the fridge for up to 5 days or in the freezer for up to 3 months.

Peppermint Bark

Every Christmas season, peppermint bark hits ALL the retail stores, from famous coffee chains to expensive kitchenware stores, bookstores, and more. Hot tip: Not only is it cheaper to make it at home, but it also makes for an impressive (no-bake) gift when it pops up in a holiday treat bag or box. Baking chocolate works the best in this recipe, for surefire results that don't seize.

Makes 2 dozen pieces ❄ **Prep Time: 30 minutes** ❄ **Total Time: 30 minutes plus chilling**

12 oz high-quality semisweet baking chocolate, broken into bite-sized pieces

12 oz high-quality white baking chocolate, broken into bite-sized pieces

½ tsp peppermint extract

10 standard-sized candy canes, crushed into pieces of various sizes

1. Line a 13- × 9-inch pan with parchment paper, smoothing out any wrinkles and leaving enough overhang at either end to use as handles.

2. Place the semisweet chocolate in a large microwave-safe glass measuring cup. Microwave on medium power in 20-second increments, stirring after each, until the chocolate has almost completely melted (a few lumps are okay). Stir until completely melted and smooth.

3. Pour the chocolate into the prepared pan, spreading it into a thin, even layer. Refrigerate for 15 minutes or until almost set. The chocolate should be soft enough that the next layer of chocolate will stick to it, but set enough that it won't move. Remove from the fridge.

4. Melt the white chocolate, using the method in step 2. Stir in the peppermint extract.

5. Pour the white chocolate over the semisweet chocolate in a thin, even layer, making sure not to disturb the layer underneath. Using a rubber spatula, gently spread it out in an even layer, trying not to swirl the chocolates together. Sprinkle the crushed candy canes over top in an even layer. Refrigerate until completely hardened, about 30 minutes.

6. Remove the bark from the fridge and use a knife to break it into 24 pieces.

7. Store in an airtight container in layers, with parchment or waxed paper between each layer, at room temperature for up to 5 days or in the freezer for up to 3 months.

CRISPY DATE NUT BALLS

Also known as frying pan cookies or dingbats, these fabulous treats are essentially a jazzed-up filling from date squares mixed with crispy rice cereal, then coated in coconut—perfect for date lovers! Make sure to use chopped baking dates that come packaged in a block. Dates that are packaged whole can include oils meant to prevent them from sticking to each other; they tend to not work as well in baking.

Makes 2 dozen pieces ❄ **Prep Time: 20 minutes** ❄ **Total Time: 30 minutes plus chilling**

1 cup packed brown sugar

1 cup chopped baking dates

2 eggs, beaten

½ tsp salt

1 Tbsp salted butter

1 tsp vanilla extract

2 cups crispy rice cereal

1 cup chopped pecans or other nut of choice

2 cups sweetened flaked coconut

1. In a large, heavy-bottomed skillet, combine the brown sugar, dates, eggs, and salt. Bring to a boil over medium heat, stirring constantly. Boil, stirring, until thickened, about 5 minutes.

2. Remove from the heat and stir in the butter and vanilla. Stir in the cereal and pecans until combined.

3. Line a large baking sheet with parchment or waxed paper.

4. Pour the coconut onto a plate. Using a tablespoon-sized cookie scoop, scoop up a heaping portion of dough (about 2 tablespoons) and drop it into the coconut. Roll in the coconut, shaping the dough into a 1½-inch ball and ensuring it is completely coated with coconut. Place on the baking sheet. Repeat with the remaining dough. Refrigerate until firm, about 15 minutes.

5. Store in an airtight container in layers, with parchment or waxed paper between each layer, in the fridge for up to 5 days or in the freezer for up to 3 months.

Chocolate-Covered Peanut Butter Balls

These classic no-bake treats are a chocolate peanut butter lover's dream come true. You can keep them plain or embrace other specialties: top them with Christmas sprinkles for extra festive flair, or with sea salt (my top choice) or peanuts for an extra-crunchy texture.

Makes 5 dozen pieces ❄ Prep Time: 30 minutes ❄ Total Time: 30 minutes plus chilling

2 cups smooth peanut butter (not natural)

¾ cup + 2 Tbsp salted butter, divided

1 tsp vanilla extract

5–6 cups icing sugar, sifted

4 cups semisweet chocolate chips

½ cup chopped peanuts, sprinkles, or sea salt flakes, for topping (optional)

1. Line two large baking sheets with parchment paper.

2. In a stand mixer with the paddle attachment or in a large bowl using a handheld mixer, beat the peanut butter, ¾ cup of the butter, and vanilla on low speed until smooth. With the mixer on low speed, add the icing sugar, 1 cup at a time, adding just enough to form a firm dough that you can roll, doesn't stick to your hands too much, and will hold its shape in a ball. Refrigerate for 30 minutes.

3. Roll the dough into 1-inch balls and place on the prepared baking sheets. Place in the freezer until firm, about 90 minutes.

4. Place the chocolate chips and the remaining 2 tablespoons butter in a large microwave-safe glass measuring cup. Microwave on medium power in 20-second increments, stirring after each, until the chocolate chips have almost completely melted (a few lumps are okay). Stir until melted, combined, and smooth.

5. Remove one baking sheet from the freezer. Place each frozen peanut butter ball flat on a fork (do not pierce) and dip into the melted chocolate, coating completely. Let the excess drip off, then return to the baking sheet. Immediately sprinkle with your topping of choice (if using). Repeat with the balls on the second sheet. Refrigerate until the chocolate has set.

6. Store in an airtight container in layers, with parchment or waxed paper between each layer, in the fridge for up to 5 days or in the freezer for up to 3 months.

CHOCOLATE TRUFFLES

Chocolate truffles might be a little finicky, but in essence, all they are is a perfect no-bake chocolate confection made from a 2:1 ratio of chocolate and cream. You can adjust this recipe to yield a larger batch, keeping that ratio in mind. I love these made with mint extract, but vanilla is always a solid choice, and if you want to go wild, try orange extract to mimic those chocolate oranges found in many stockings come Christmas morning!

Makes 15 pieces ❄ **Prep Time: 30 minutes** ❄ **Total Time: 35 minutes plus chilling**

½ cup whipping cream or heavy cream

8 oz semisweet baking chocolate, coarsely chopped

1 tsp extract of choice (such as mint, vanilla, or orange)

Unsweetened cocoa powder, finely chopped nuts, finely shredded sweetened coconut, or sprinkles, for coating

1. In a small saucepan over medium heat, heat the cream, stirring, until hot but not boiling.

2. Remove from the heat and stir in the chocolate. Let stand until the chocolate softens, then stir until well combined. Stir in the extract. Let cool, then refrigerate until cold, about 2 hours.

3. Line a large baking sheet with parchment or waxed paper.

4. Form a tablespoonful of the chocolate mixture into a ball and place on the prepared baking sheet. Try to handle as little and lightly as possible, or it will start to melt! Repeat with the remaining chocolate mixture. Refrigerate for 30 minutes.

5. Pour the desired coating onto a plate. Quickly reshape any balls as needed, then roll the balls in the coating and return to the baking sheet. Refrigerate for another 30 minutes.

6. Store in an airtight container in layers, with parchment or waxed paper between each later, in the fridge for up to 1 week or in the freezer for up to 3 months.

Crushed Cookie Truffles

This recipe is the easiest Christmas no-bake hack ever. All you need is six ingredients, and the type of cookies and extract can be swapped out to create different taste combinations. Make sure to take advantage of all the Oreo cookie varieties that come out around Christmas—they work the best in this recipe and come in the most amazing holiday flavors!

Makes 3 dozen pieces ❄ **Prep Time: 15 minutes** ❄ **Total Time: 15 minutes plus chilling**

1 package (8 oz/226 g) cream cheese, softened

36 mint cream–filled cookies (such as Oreos), finely crushed

8 oz semisweet baking chocolate, coarsely chopped

2 Tbsp salted butter

½ tsp mint extract

Crushed candy canes, for topping

1. Line a large baking sheet with parchment paper.

2. In a bowl, mix together the cream cheese and cookie crumbs until well combined.

3. Using a tablespoon-sized cookie scoop, scoop up the cream cheese mixture and shape into 1-inch balls, placing them on the prepared baking sheet. Place in the freezer for 20 minutes.

4. Place the chocolate and butter in a large microwave-safe glass measuring cup. Microwave on medium power in 20-second increments, stirring after each, until the chocolate has almost completely melted (a few lumps are okay). Stir until fully melted, combined, and smooth. Stir in the mint extract.

5. Remove the baking sheet from the freezer. Place each dough ball flat on a fork (do not pierce) and dip into the melted chocolate, coating completely. Let the excess drip off, then return to the baking sheet. Immediately sprinkle with the crushed candy canes before the chocolate sets. Refrigerate for 60 minutes or until firm.

6. Store in an airtight container in a single layer, or with parchment or waxed paper between each layer, in the fridge for up to 1 week or in the freezer for up to 3 months.

CLASSIC RUM BALLS

Those who own my first cookbook will know my journey with these tasty treats. I have loved rum balls my entire life! I was that kid who would always pick the rum balls first on the dainty tray at Christmas—odd, since now, as an adult, I don't prefer rum in my cocktails. However, the fantastic flavor combination of chocolate and rum is still my go-to when it comes to desserts!

Makes 4 dozen pieces ❄ **Prep Time: 30 minutes** ❄ **Total Time: 1 hour**

1½ cups butter

3 cups granulated sugar

1½ cups unsweetened
   cocoa powder

6 eggs, beaten

1½ cups flour

½ cup dark rum

¼ cup sweetened
   condensed milk

1½ cups chocolate sprinkles

1. Preheat the oven to 350°F. Line a 13- × 9-inch pan with parchment paper.

2. In a large saucepan over medium heat, melt the butter. Remove from the heat and add the sugar, stirring to dissolve as much as possible. (There's a lot more sugar than butter, so it might not all dissolve.) Stir in the cocoa until well combined. Add the eggs and mix until thoroughly combined. Stir in the flour until just mixed in—do not overmix.

3. Pour the batter into the prepared pan.

4. Bake for 30 to 35 minutes or until the edges start to pull away from the sides of the pan and the center is still slightly underbaked. Let cool completely in the pan, then break the cake into pieces.

5. In a stand mixer with the paddle attachment or in a large bowl using a handheld mixer, mix the cake pieces, rum, and milk on low speed until a cakey dough forms.

6. Pour the chocolate sprinkles onto a plate. Roll the dough into 1-inch balls, then roll in the chocolate sprinkles to coat.

7. Store in an airtight container in a single layer, or with parchment or waxed paper between each layer, in the fridge for up to 5 days or in the freezer for up to 3 months.

Chocolate Haystacks

The no-bake haystack cookies I grew up with were always a chocolate-butterscotch flavor combination, and I have to say, I stand by that! With that said for keeping it classic, feel free to play around with the type of chocolate (Why not try dark or white?). However, the type of chow mein noodles matters: they must be the crispy cooked ones, like the brand Farkay. These are thicker than most cooked chow mein noodles, and hold up the best when baked for this treat.

Makes 2 dozen pieces ❄ **Prep Time: 20 minutes** ❄ **Total Time: 20 minutes plus chilling**

1 bag (10 oz/300 g) semisweet chocolate chips

1 bag (10 oz/300 g) butterscotch baking chips

5 cups crispy cooked chow mein noodles (such as Farkay)

1. Line a large baking sheet with parchment or waxed paper.

2. Place the chocolate and butterscotch chips in a large microwave-safe glass measuring cup. Microwave on medium power in 20-second increments, stirring after each, until the chips have almost completely melted (a few lumps are okay). Stir until fully melted, combined, and smooth.

3. Place the noodles in a large bowl. Pour the melted chocolate mixture over top, mixing gently to coat the noodles completely.

4. Drop by heaping tablespoonfuls onto the prepared baking sheet, spacing them 1½ inches apart. Refrigerate until set, about 15 minutes.

5. Store in an airtight container in layers, with parchment or waxed paper between each layer, in the fridge for up to 1 week or in the freezer for up to 3 months.

PEANUT BUTTERSCOTCH CEREAL CLUSTERS

These were one of my all-time favorite treats growing up! My mom reminded me that she used to make them every Christmas in the 1980s—she's not sure why she stopped—and as soon as she said this, I got flashbacks of the dessert trays in our large '70s-era house, with its classic sunken living room and wall-to-wall stone fireplace where we hung our stockings, and the Christmas I received my very first Cabbage Patch Doll. (If you're a child of the '80s, you'll be able to tell me when you got your first CPD!) Now these no-bake clusters are back on my yearly Christmas baking list. As with the Chocolate Haystacks on page 159, you can play around with the type of baking chips you use, and even switch out the peanuts for raisins if you're feeling especially adventurous.

Makes 2 dozen pieces ❄ **Prep Time: 20 minutes** ❄ **Total Time: 20 minutes plus chilling**

1 bag (10 oz/300 g) butterscotch baking chips

1 cup smooth peanut butter (not natural)

4 cups plain O-shaped cereal (such as Cheerios)

1 cup salted dry-roasted peanuts

1. Line a large baking sheet with parchment or waxed paper.

2. Place the butterscotch chips and peanut butter in a large microwave-safe glass measuring cup. Microwave on medium power in 20-second increments, stirring after each, until the butterscotch has almost completely melted (a few lumps are okay). Stir until fully melted, combined, and smooth.

3. Place the cereal and peanuts in a large bowl. Pour the melted butterscotch mixture over top, mixing gently to coat the cereal and peanuts completely.

4. Drop by heaping tablespoonfuls onto the prepared baking sheet, spacing them 1½ inches apart. Refrigerate until set, about 15 minutes.

5. Store in an airtight container in layers, with parchment or waxed paper between each layer, at room temperature for up to 5 days or in the freezer for up to 3 months.

Dad's Coconut Caramel Corn Cereal Treats

These amazing chewy, caramel-filled treats are my dad's favorite concoction. (I know where my sweet tooth comes from!) My dad is very good in the kitchen when inspired (this is actually his recipe), so it's his job at Christmas to make a batch of these. If you're not a big coconut fan, you can use an additional cup of cereal instead. But the flaked coconut turns these into super-chewy jaw-busters, which is what makes them so darn good.

Makes 2 dozen pieces ❄ Prep Time: 20 minutes ❄ Total Time: 20 minutes

½ cup salted butter

¼ cup whipping cream or heavy cream

½ tsp vanilla extract

50 caramels, unwrapped

5 cups unsweetened cornflakes cereal

1 cup sweetened flaked coconut

1. Line a large baking sheet with parchment or waxed paper.

2. Place the butter, cream, vanilla, and caramels in a large saucepan over low heat. Stir, melting the caramels, until all the ingredients are combined. Be careful not to boil or cook.

3. Remove from the heat and stir in the cereal and coconut until completely coated.

4. Drop by heaping tablespoonfuls onto the prepared baking sheet, spacing them 1½ inches apart. Let cool and set at room temperature, about 30 minutes.

5. Store in an airtight container in layers, with parchment or waxed paper between each layer, at room temperature for up to 5 days or in the freezer for up to 3 months.

NO-BAKE CARAMEL GRAHAM MARSHMALLOW DROPS

Is it even Christmas on the Prairies if at least three dainties you're presenting on a lovely tray don't star mini marshmallows and coconut? I've given these vintage treats a new flavor profile with the addition of dulce de leche, a caramel-flavored condensed milk, sometimes labeled "dulce de leche sauce" on the can. For the ultimate traditional taste, sub in plain unsweetened condensed milk. These treats are perfect for snacking on straight from the freezer—no need to thaw! They are so chewy when frozen!

Makes 2 dozen pieces ❄ Prep Time: 30 minutes ❄ Total Time: 30 minutes plus chilling

2 cups graham cracker crumbs

1 can (13.4 oz or 300 mL) dulce de leche

½ tsp vanilla extract

2 cups mini marshmallows

½ cup chopped red and green glace cherries (optional, see tip)

2 cups unsweetened shredded coconut

1. Line a large baking sheet with parchment paper.

2. In a large bowl, combine the graham crumbs, dulce de leche, and vanilla, stirring until thoroughly combined and there are no dry crumbs left. Stir in the marshmallows and cherries (if using) until evenly distributed.

3. Pour the coconut onto a large plate. Roll the graham mixture into 1-inch balls, then roll in the coconut until coated. Place on the prepared baking sheet. Refrigerate until firm, about 20 minutes.

4. Store in an airtight container in layers, with parchment or waxed paper between each layer, at room temperature for up to 1 week or in the freezer for up to 3 months.

TIP:

In place of the glace cherries, you can use chopped toasted pecans or walnuts (see page 59), or drained and chopped maraschino cherries.

CHAPTER FIVE

DAINTIES, BARS & SLICES

Remember at the beginning of this book when I said I could have included 250 recipes? Bars and slices would've made up most of them—there are more varieties than you can imagine!

But I behaved myself. I whittled it down to the best of the best, from tried-and-true staples to tasty new takes. They had to be easy, delicious, and popular, so I knew the 7-Layer Bars (page 174) were a given. Try both versions: I gave the classic Hello Dolly bars a Christmas glow-up—which I actually enjoy more (unsurprising, given that I manage to stretch Christmas decor and celebrations out to almost two months of the year).

I also had to include Canadian classics like the Nanaimo Bars (page 181), and I couldn't not share my perfected Lemon Bars (page 186).

These all freeze well, with the exception of the Puffed Wheat Squares (page 203). But treats like the Marshmallow Yule Logs (page 170) are so wildly popular for Christmas because they can be made ahead of time and frozen without the quality suffering in the slightest. Over the years, I've learned two major tips for storing frozen treats. First, always let your treat cool completely before freezing. If you put warm bars in the freezer, the heat builds up extra moisture and you'll get frost flakes all over them.

Then the perennial question: To slice or not to slice? For gooier goods, like the Lemon Bars (page 186) and the Butter Tart Bars (page 193), freeze them in the pan until they are firm, but not completely frozen, then slice and stack in layers before returning them to the freezer. My sister takes a different approach: she likes to slice the entire pan in half, then place each half in its own freezer-safe bag and lay them flat to freeze. Storage-wise, that also works like a charm, but it's hard to snack on a few bars at a time when they're frozen in one large, solid piece . . . and why not dip into your bar stash throughout the year?

Mint Chocolate Dainties

A traditional mint chocolate dainty base has nuts, coconut, and raw egg, but I wanted to make a version that more people would enjoy (coconut haters, this one is especially for you!), so I've used cookie crumbs instead. This is another recipe where you can switch up the type of cream-filled cookies you use: try the ones with mint filling, the all-chocolate type, or even the coffee-flavored ones.

Makes 4 dozen squares ❊ Prep Time: 30 minutes ❊ Total Time: 30 minutes plus chilling

CHOCOLATE CRUST

38 cream-filled cookies, finely chopped (I like Oreos)

¾ cup salted butter

½ cup semisweet chocolate chips

¼ tsp mint extract

MINT FILLING

⅔ cup salted butter, softened

3 cups icing sugar

¼ cup whipping cream or heavy cream

1½ tsp mint extract

4–5 drops green food coloring

CHOCOLATE TOPPING

1⅓ cups semisweet chocolate chips

¼ cup salted butter

⅛ tsp mint extract

1. For the crust: Place the chopped cookies in a large bowl and set aside. Place the butter and chocolate chips in a large microwave-safe glass measuring cup. Microwave on medium power in 20-second increments, stirring after each, until the chocolate chips have almost completely melted (a few lumps are okay). Stir until fully melted, combined, and smooth. Stir in the mint extract until fully combined, then pour over the cookies and stir until fully incorporated.

2. Press the crust mixture firmly into the bottom of an ungreased 13- × 9-inch pan. Refrigerate for 10 minutes.

3. For the filling: Meanwhile, in a stand mixer with the paddle attachment or in a large bowl using a handheld mixer, beat the butter and icing sugar on medium speed until smooth. Beat in the cream and mint extract. Beat in enough food coloring to reach your desired color.

4. Spread the filling evenly over the crust. Refrigerate for 2 hours or until set.

5. For the topping: Place the chocolate chips and butter in a large microwave-safe glass measuring cup. Microwave on medium power in 20-second increments, stirring after each, until the chocolate chips have almost completely melted (a few lumps are okay). Stir until fully melted, combined, and smooth. Stir in the mint extract. Let cool as much as possible while remaining liquid.

6. Spread the topping evenly over the filling. Refrigerate for 60 minutes, then slice into 48 squares.

7. Store in an airtight container in layers, with parchment or waxed paper between each layer, in the fridge for up to 1 week or in the freezer for up to 3 months.

MARSHMALLOW YULE LOGS

The prettiest Christmas dainty of all! Very old versions of these yule logs are called TV rolls and include a raw egg yolk, but it's not actually needed—luckily, since most of us are hesitant to use raw eggs in recipes nowadays. It works perfectly fine without that old-fashioned addition. If coconut isn't your thing, you can roll the logs in chopped nuts instead.

Makes 2 dozen slices ❄ **Prep Time: 20 minutes** ❄ **Total Time: 20 minutes plus chilling**

2 cups semisweet chocolate chips

½ cup salted butter

5½ cups rainbow mini marshmallows

1 cup chopped walnuts

1 cup sweetened flaked coconut or chopped nuts (such as walnuts or hazelnuts)

1. Place the chocolate chips and butter in a medium microwave-safe glass measuring cup. Microwave in 20-second increments, stirring after each until the chocolate chips have almost completely melted (a few lumps are okay). Stir until fully melted, combined, and smooth. Let cool until just warm, but not so hot as to melt the marshmallows in the next step.

2. Place the marshmallows and walnuts in a large bowl. Pour in the chocolate mixture, stirring to coat completely. Let cool.

3. Spread the coconut on a sheet of waxed paper. Divide the marshmallow mixture into 2 equal pieces and roll each into a 4-inch-long log. Place 1 log on the coconut, fold the waxed paper over it, and roll back and forth to coat the log. (I do this without touching the log with my hands, as the mixture is sticky!) Wrap the log in a new piece of waxed paper, then in plastic wrap. Repeat with the second log.

4. Store the wrapped logs in an airtight container in the fridge for up to 1 week or in the freezer for up to 3 months.

5. To serve, thaw (if necessary) until still chilled and firm but sliceable, then cut each log into 12 slices.

Marshmallow Peanut Rolls

This is the homemade version of a popular candy bar we have only found in the US, with creamy vanilla nougat filling surrounded by caramel and crushed peanuts. Now you can make it at home, no matter where you live! This recipe takes practice and a lot of time, but is totally worth it!

Makes 72 slices ❄ Prep Time: 1 hour ❄ Total Time: 1 hour plus chilling

4 cups mini marshmallows

¾ cup + 2 Tbsp salted butter, divided

2 tsp vanilla extract

4 cups sifted icing sugar (approx.), plus more for dusting

50 caramels, unwrapped

3 Tbsp whipping cream or heavy cream

2½ cups salted dry-roasted peanuts, coarsely chopped (see tip)

TIP:
You can also switch out the peanuts for pecans.

1. Line a baking sheet with parchment or waxed paper.

2. Place the marshmallows and ¾ cup of the butter in a medium saucepan. Heat over medium heat, stirring until melted, combined, and smooth.

3. Remove from the heat and stir in the vanilla. Stir in the icing sugar until fully incorporated. Let the nougat cool until you can safely touch it.

4. On a work surface lightly dusted with sifted icing sugar, knead the nougat, adding small amounts of icing sugar as needed, until it has firmed up and is dull, not shiny. Divide the nougat into 6 equal pieces and roll each into a log about 6 inches long and 1 inch in diameter. Place on the prepared baking sheet. Stick a toothpick in the top of each log at each end, to use for dipping later. Brush off all excess icing sugar. Place in the freezer for 2 hours.

5. Place the caramels, cream, and the remaining 2 tablespoons butter in a large saucepan. Heat over low heat, stirring occasionally, until melted, combined, and smooth. Do NOT bring to a boil or overheat. Turn down the heat to the lowest setting to keep warm.

6. Place the peanuts on a large baking sheet. Using the toothpicks, lift 1 log and dip it into the caramel, coating it completely. Let the excess caramel drip off, then place the log on top of the peanuts. Remove the toothpicks and roll the log in the peanuts, coating the caramel, making sure the shape stays a cylinder. Return the coated log to the lined baking sheet. Repeat with the remaining logs. Refrigerate for 1 hour.

7. Wrap each log in plastic wrap and store in an airtight container in the fridge for up to 1 week or in the freezer for up to 3 months.

8. To serve a roll, bring it to room temperature, then cut into 12 slices.

7-LAYER BARS

Also known as Hello Dolly bars, these are probably the sweetest bars ever invented, with seven layers of flavor! The classic recipe below is the one everyone is used to, but I also have a Christmas version I like to make because I adore using red and green glace cherries for the holidays—I put them in everything I possibly can! I use unsweetened coconut to cut the tooth-aching sweetness, but if you prefer to keep it traditional (with all the intended sweetness), feel free to use sweetened.

Makes 30 bars ✳ **Prep Time: 15 minutes** ✳ **Total Time: 45 minutes**

1¾ cups graham cracker crumbs

½ cup melted salted butter

1 can (14 oz or 300 mL) sweetened condensed milk

1 cup semisweet chocolate chips

1 cup butterscotch baking chips

1 cup chopped walnuts, almonds, or pecans

1½ cups unsweetened shredded coconut

1. Preheat the oven to 350°F. Line a 13- × 9-inch baking pan with foil, then grease the foil with cooking spray.

2. In a small bowl, combine the crumbs and butter, mixing until the crumbs are well coated.

3. Press the crumb mixture evenly into the bottom of the prepared pan. Pour the condensed milk over top in an even layer. Sprinkle the remaining ingredients over top, in the order noted, pressing them into the milk layer.

4. Bake for 25 to 30 minutes or until the coconut is browned. Let cool completely in the pan, then slice into 30 bars.

5. Store in an airtight container in layers, with parchment or waxed paper between each layer, at room temperature for up to 5 days or in the freezer for up to 3 months.

CHRISTMAS VARIATION

* Use chocolate baking crumbs instead of the graham cracker crumbs.
* Use dulce de leche , a caramel-flavored condensed milk (sometimes labeled "dulce de leche sauce" on the can), instead of the sweetened condensed milk.
* Use chopped red and green glace cherries instead of the butterscotch baking chips.

Marshmallow Bars

From rainbow marshmallows paired with butterscotch to the chocolate-and-peanut beauty that is Rocky Road, marshmallow bars can be made using so many different flavors, and as a bonus, they are the easiest bars you can make! The number of marshmallows you use in these bars can vary: some people like them more fudge than marshmallow; others like them way fluffier, until they're basically one big marshmallow held together by fudge. I've suggested measurements based on each variation's star ingredients, but feel free to experiment with more or fewer marshmallows to create your perfect bar. Whichever version calls to you, all follow the same method, so making marshmallow magic couldn't be simpler.

Makes 2 dozen bars ⁂ Prep Time: 15 minutes ⁂ Total Time: 15 minutes plus chilling

BUTTERSCOTCH RAINBOW

1 cup smooth peanut butter (not natural)

½ cup salted butter

1 bag (10 oz/300 g) butterscotch baking chips

½ tsp vanilla extract

6–8 cups rainbow mini marshmallows

ROCKY ROAD

1 cup chunky peanut butter (not natural)

½ cup salted butter

1 bag (10 oz/300 g) semisweet chocolate chips

½ tsp vanilla extract

6 cups white mini marshmallows

1 cup chopped peanuts

HAZELNUT RAINBOW BARS

1 cup chocolate hazelnut spread (such as Nutella)

½ cup salted butter

1 bag (10 oz/300 g) semisweet chocolate chips

½ tsp vanilla extract

6–8 cups rainbow mini marshmallows

½–1 cup chopped toasted hazelnuts

FULLY LOADED MARSHMALLOW BARS (HOLD MY BEER, HERE WE GO)

1 cup chunky peanut butter (not natural)

½ cup salted butter

1 bag (10 oz/300 g) semisweet chocolate chips

½ tsp vanilla extract

4 cups white mini marshmallows

½ cup chopped peanuts

½ cup sweetened shredded coconut

½ cup crispy rice cereal

½ cup chopped well-drained maraschino cherries

see over

METHOD FOR ALL MARSHMALLOW BARS

1. Line a 13- × 9-inch pan with parchment paper.

2. Place the first three ingredients in a medium saucepan. Heat over medium heat, stirring frequently, until melted, combined, and smooth.

3. Remove from the heat and stir in the vanilla. Let cool until just warm, but not so hot as to melt the marshmallows in the next step.

4. Place the remaining ingredients in a large bowl. Pour in the peanut butter mixture, stirring to coat completely.

5. Pour into the prepared pan, spreading evenly. Refrigerate for 2 to 3 hours, then slice into 24 bars.

6. Store in an airtight container in layers, with parchment or waxed paper between each layer, in the fridge for up to 5 days or in the freezer for up to 3 months.

CLASSIC CANADIAN NANAIMO BARS

Everybody who makes Nanaimo bars has their preferred recipe, whether they're looking for a thin-bottomed bar with a monster-thick filling, or a thin filling to top a thick base. As you might remember from my first book, our family's classic version is grounded with a slightly thicker base, with a solid filling and a generous layer of chocolate on top. It just doesn't get any better than that!

Makes 20 bars ❄ Prep Time: 30 minutes ❄ Total Time: 40 minutes plus chilling

BOTTOM LAYER

⅓ cup salted butter, melted

¼ cup granulated sugar

1¼ cups graham cracker crumbs

½ cup sweetened shredded coconut

⅓ cup unsweetened cocoa powder

⅓ cup finely chopped walnuts

1 egg, lightly beaten

MIDDLE LAYER

2 cups icing sugar

½ cup butter, softened

3 Tbsp whipping cream or heavy cream

2 Tbsp custard powder

TOP LAYER

1 cup semisweet chocolate chips

2 Tbsp salted butter

1. Preheat the oven to 350°F. Line a 9-inch square pan with parchment paper.

2. For the bottom layer: In a medium bowl, mix the butter and granulated sugar until the sugar starts to dissolve. Mix in the graham crumbs, coconut, cocoa, and walnuts until combined. Add the egg, mixing well.

3. Press the graham mixture firmly into the bottom of the prepared pan.

4. Bake for 10 minutes. Let cool completely.

5. For the middle layer: In a stand mixer with the paddle attachment or in a large bowl using a handheld mixer, beat together the icing sugar, butter, cream, and custard powder on medium speed. Spread evenly over the bottom layer.

6. For the top layer: Place the chocolate chips and butter in a large microwave-safe glass measuring cup. Microwave on medium power in 20-second intervals, stirring after each, until the chocolate chips have almost completely melted (a few lumps are okay). Stir until fully melted, combined, and smooth. Spread evenly over the middle layer.

7. Refrigerate for 2 hours, then slice into 20 bars. Nanaimo bars are best when served chilled, as the center is basically cream and butter!

8. Store in an airtight container in layers, with parchment or waxed paper between each layer, in the fridge for up to 5 days or in the freezer for up to 3 months.

Pecan Toffee Bars

Every Christmas season, my family makes these toffee bars, and every season they are a hit. Walnuts make a great substitute for the topping. For nut-free households, these are just as delicious without any nuts on top.

Makes 4 dozen bars ❄ Prep Time: 15 minutes ❄ Total Time: 40 minutes plus chilling

BASE

2 cups flour

1 cup salted butter, softened

½ cup icing sugar

FILLING

1 cup sweetened condensed milk

¾ cup packed brown sugar

½ cup salted butter

3 Tbsp light corn syrup

TOPPING

48 toasted pecan or walnut halves (optional; see tip, page 59)

1. Preheat the oven to 350°F.

2. For the base: In a medium bowl, using your hands or a pastry blender, crumble together the flour, butter, and icing sugar.

3. Press the base mixture firmly into the bottom of an ungreased 13 × 9-inch pan.

4. Bake for 20 minutes or until the base is set and lightly browned. Let cool completely.

5. For the filling: In a small, heavy-bottomed saucepan, combine the milk, brown sugar, butter, and corn syrup. Bring to a boil over medium heat, stirring constantly. Boil for 5 minutes, continuing to stir and ensuring the mixture doesn't burn.

6. Remove from the heat and beat with a wooden spoon until the filling starts to thicken. Pour over the base.

7. For the topping: Arrange the pecans over the filling, spaced out in rows of 6 by 8 pecans.

8. Refrigerate until completely set, about 2 hours, then slice into 48 bars.

9. Store in an airtight container in layers, with parchment or waxed paper between each layer, at room temperature for up to 5 days or in the freezer for up to 3 months.

PEANUT BUTTER BARS

I've never understood why at Christmas (the busiest time of year for me, both website- and family-wise) my first thought is "Hey, I'm going to try to replicate all the store-bought treats at home!" Maybe it's the desire to save money, or perhaps it's because it's simply darn fun, but it's one of the baking challenges I most enjoy during the holiday season. Here's another recipe for a beloved store-bought treat. Because they have no preservatives, they must be kept refrigerated for the best texture.

Makes 2 dozen bars ❄ **Prep Time: 20 minutes** ❄ **Total Time: 20 minutes plus chilling**

PEANUT BUTTER BASE

2 cups graham cracker crumbs

1½ cups icing sugar

1 cup packed brown sugar

1 cup melted salted butter

1 cup smooth peanut butter (not natural)

½ tsp vanilla extract

CHOCOLATE PEANUT BUTTER TOPPING

2 cups semisweet chocolate chips

¼ cup smooth peanut butter

1. For the base: In a medium bowl, mix together all the base ingredients until well blended.

2. Press the base mixture evenly into the bottom of an ungreased 13- × 9-inch pan. Refrigerate for 30 minutes.

3. For the topping: Place the chocolate chips and peanut butter in a large microwave-safe glass measuring cup. Microwave on medium power in 20-second increments, stirring after each, until completely melted, combined, and smooth.

4. Pour the topping over the base, spreading it out gently into an even layer. Refrigerate until set, about 1 hour, then slice into 24 bars.

5. Store in an airtight container in layers, with parchment or waxed paper between each layer, in the fridge for up to 5 days or in the freezer for up to 3 months.

Lemon Bars

Nothing beats a good lemon bar for the holidays, so here it is: my perfected recipe! These don't get soggy, and they have a firm filling that freezes beautifully for enjoying months down the line. Adding some lemon zest to the shortbread crust really makes them pop with flavor. These should be kept refrigerated so that the bars stay firm.

Makes 20 bars ❄ **Prep Time: 20 minutes** ❄ **Total Time: 1 hour, 5 minutes**

SHORTBREAD CRUST

2 cups flour

1 cup icing sugar

¼ cup cornstarch

1 cup salted butter, softened

1 Tbsp lemon zest

LEMON FILLING

3 cups granulated sugar

¾ cup flour

¾ cup lemon juice

¼ tsp salt

6 eggs, beaten well

Icing sugar, for sprinkling

1. Preheat the oven to 350°F. Line a 13- × 9-inch pan with parchment paper, leaving enough overhang at either end to use as handles.

2. For the crust: In a medium bowl, using a pastry blender or by crisscrossing two knives, mix together all the crust ingredients until the butter is incorporated and the mixture resembles coarse crumbs.

3. Press the crust mixture evenly into the bottom of the prepared pan.

4. Bake for 15 to 20 minutes or until firm and golden brown. Remove from the oven, leaving the oven on.

5. For the filling: In a large bowl, whisk together all the filling ingredients until smooth and completely combined. Pour over the baked crust.

6. Bake for 20 to 25 minutes or until the filling starts to set, but do not let brown! The bars will firm up as they cool down. Let cool completely in the pan. Sprinkle with icing sugar, then slice into 20 bars.

7. Store in an airtight container in layers, with parchment or waxed paper between each layer, in the fridge for up to 5 days or in the freezer for up to 3 months.

MARMALADE BARS

Cakey and perfect for marmalade lovers, these are a cheery burst of citrus flavor when you are smack-dab in the middle of winter. If desired, you can add a teaspoon or two of lemon zest along with the orange zest to really make the citrus pop!

Makes 15 bars ❄ **Prep Time: 20 minutes** ❄ **Total Time: 1 hour, 5 minutes**

2 cups flour

1 cup rolled oats

1 cup granulated sugar

1 Tbsp orange zest

1–2 tsp lemon zest (optional)

1 tsp baking powder

1 tsp salt

1 tsp ground cinnamon

¼ tsp ground cloves

¼ tsp ground nutmeg

1 cup butter, cold and cut into cubes

2 eggs

½ cup orange juice

¼ tsp almond extract

1½ cups orange marmalade

1. Preheat the oven to 350°F. Butter a 9-inch square pan.

2. In a large bowl, whisk together the flour, oats, sugar, orange zest, lemon zest (if using), baking powder, salt, cinnamon, cloves, and nutmeg. Using a pastry blender or by crisscrossing two knives, cut in the butter until it is the size of lentils.

3. In a spouted measuring cup, beat together the eggs, orange juice, and almond extract. Pour into the flour mixture, stirring with a wooden spoon until well combined.

4. Spoon half of the batter into the prepared pan and spread into an even layer, pressing it down into the pan. Spread the marmalade over top in an even layer. Drop the remaining batter over top in pieces to cover the marmalade.

5. Bake for 40 to 45 minutes or until the top is browned and slightly crispy. Let cool completely in the pan, then slice into 15 bars.

6. Store in an airtight container in layers, with parchment or waxed paper between each layer, at room temperature for up to 5 days or in the freezer for up to 3 months.

Coconut Jam Bars

The lovely thing about these shortbread bars is how easy they are to customize! I like them best with walnuts and raspberry jam, but you could just as easily (and deliciously) use blueberry or cherry jam and replace the walnuts with slivered almonds. These were one of my grandma's favorite dainties; she kept a stash in her freezer year-round for teatime.

Makes 15 bars ❄ **Prep Time: 10 minutes** ❄ **Total Time: 45 minutes**

2 cups flour

¼ tsp salt

¼ tsp baking powder

¾ cup butter, softened

½ cup granulated sugar

½ cup packed brown sugar

1 egg

1 tsp vanilla extract

2 cups sweetened shredded coconut, divided

¾ cup finely chopped walnuts

1½ cups raspberry jam

½ cup chopped walnuts

1. Preheat the oven to 350°F. Butter a 13- × 9-inch pan.

2. In a medium bowl, whisk together the flour, salt, and baking powder. Set aside.

3. In a stand mixer with the paddle attachment or in a large bowl using a handheld mixer, beat the butter, granulated sugar, and brown sugar on high speed until smooth and creamy, about 2 minutes. Add the egg, beating well. Mix in the vanilla until combined. With the mixer on low speed, gradually add the flour mixture, mixing until fully incorporated. Using a wooden spoon, stir in 1 cup of the coconut and the finely chopped walnuts until evenly distributed.

4. Press two-thirds of the dough evenly into the bottom of the prepared pan. Spread the jam over the dough. Sprinkle with the remaining 1 cup coconut and the chopped walnuts. Crumble the remaining dough into small pieces over top, then press down gently.

5. Bake for 30 to 35 minutes or until the topping is golden brown. Let cool completely in the pan, then slice into 15 bars.

6. Store in an airtight container in layers, with parchment or waxed paper between each layer, at room temperature for up to 5 days or in the freezer for up to 3 months.

BUTTER TART BARS

These butter tart bars are almost as easy as homemade butter tarts using store-bought tart shells, with a lovely shortbread crust instead. You can whip these up in no time at all, and they are just as delicious as real butter tarts!

Makes 24 bars ⁜ **Prep Time: 15 minutes** ⁜ **Total Time: 50 minutes**

CRUST

1¼ cups flour

⅓ cup packed brown sugar

½ cup butter

TOPPING

2 eggs, beaten

1 cup packed brown sugar

1½ cups raisins

½ cup chopped nuts (optional)

¼ cup butter

1 tsp flour

½ tsp baking powder

¼ tsp salt

1 tsp vanilla extract

1. Preheat oven to 350°F.

2. For the crust: In a medium bowl, mix together all the crust ingredients until crumbly.

3. Press the crust mixture evenly into the bottom of an ungreased 9-inch square pan.

4. Bake for about 15 minutes or until browned. Remove from the oven, leaving the oven on.

5. For the topping: In a large bowl, mix together the eggs and brown sugar well. Add the remaining ingredients and mix until well combined. Pour over the crust.

6. Bake for 18 to 20 minutes or until beautifully browned. Let cool completely in the pan, then slice into 24 bars.

7. Store in an airtight container in layers, with parchment or waxed paper between each layer, in the fridge for up to 5 days or in the freezer for up to 3 months.

Butter Tarts

My butter tarts are my most requested treat over the holidays. Over the years, some of my friends have even offered to pay me to put together a tin or two for their Christmas night dessert—that's how good these are! The recipe was in such demand after I left it out of my first book, I shuddered to think what would happen if I left it out of this one too! While I won't skip out on making the pastry from scratch (this is a baking book, after all), you can, of course, use premade unsweetened frozen tart shells, available at any grocery store.

Makes 12 tarts ❄ Prep Time: 30 minutes ❄ Total Time: 1 hour plus chilling

QUICK BUTTER PASTRY

2½ cups flour

2 tsp granulated sugar

1 tsp salt

1 cup unsalted butter, frozen

¼–½ cup ice water

BUTTER TART FILLING

1 cup packed brown sugar

⅔ cup raisins

⅓ cup melted salted butter

2 Tbsp whipping cream or
   heavy cream

1 tsp vanilla extract

1 egg, beaten

1. For the pastry: In a large bowl, whisk together the flour, granulated sugar, and salt. Using a cheese grater, grate in the frozen butter. Using a pastry blender or by crisscrossing two knives, cut in the butter until the mixture is crumbly and the butter is the size of peas. Add the ice water, 1 tablespoon at a time, tossing with a fork to mix, until the dough stays together when pinched between your fingers.

2. Divide the dough into 2 equal pieces and form each into a disk. Wrap each disk tightly with plastic wrap and refrigerate for 1 hour.

3. Preheat the oven to 375°F.

4. On a lightly floured work surface, roll out the dough to ⅛-inch thickness (keeping the second disk in the fridge). Cut out twelve 4-inch circles, rerolling as little as possible. Place each circle in one cup of a 12-cup muffin pan.

5. For the filling: In a medium bowl, mix all the filling ingredients until well combined. Spoon into the tart shells, filling each three-quarters full.

6. Bake for 17 to 20 minutes or until the filling is bubbling and the pastry has browned. Let cool in the pan for 5 minutes, then transfer to a wire baking rack and let cool completely.

7. Store in an airtight container in layers, with parchment or waxed paper between each layer, in the fridge for up to 5 days or in the freezer for up to 3 months.

DATE SQUARES

Those who own my first book might already know our favorite family story about these date squares, also known as matrimonial squares—which is fitting for us! Mr. Magpie says he married me because I baked him a lot of date squares while we were dating. These have always been his favorite sweet treat, to the point that he has requested a pan of date squares instead of a birthday cake some years! To be fair, he's now a master at baking these for himself, and he regularly makes them at Christmas. He even shares sometimes.

Makes 2 dozen squares ❋ Prep Time: 15 minutes ❋ Total Time: 40 minutes

FILLING

12 oz pitted dates

¾ cup granulated sugar

1 cup water

BASE

1½ cups salted butter, softened

1½ cups packed brown sugar

2 cups flour

1½ tsp baking soda

2 cups rolled oats

1. Preheat the oven to 350°F.

2. For the filling: In a medium saucepan, combine the dates, granulated sugar, and water. Bring to a simmer over medium-high heat, stirring frequently. Reduce the heat to low and cook, stirring frequently, for 10 to 12 minutes or until the dates are dissolved and the mixture is smooth. Set aside.

3. For the base: In a large bowl, cream the butter and brown sugar. Whisk together the flour and baking soda, then stir into the mixture until combined. Stir in the oats, mixing in completely.

4. Press two-thirds of the base mixture evenly into the bottom of an ungreased 13- × 9-inch pan. Pour the filling over the base, spreading evenly. Sprinkle the remaining base mixture evenly over top.

5. Bake for 20 to 25 minutes or until the top is beautifully browned. Let cool completely in the pan, then slice into 24 squares.

6. Store in an airtight container in layers, with parchment or waxed paper between each layer, in the fridge for up to 5 days or in the freezer for up to 3 months.

Chocolate Bar Squares

This is my "thank heavens, fast-and-easy, no-fail, panic-because-I-forgot-I-said-yes-to-the-cookie-exchange" recipe of choice. These dessert squares have been around forever; older versions call for corn syrup, but I skip it, as it's not needed in the slightest. Simply melt your favorite creamy nougat-filled chocolate bars (Mars, Milky Way, or 3 Musketeers) with butter, then mix in your favorite crispy rice cereal, cover with chocolate, and there you go: cookie exchange saved.

Makes 2 dozen squares ❄ **Prep Time: 10 minutes** ❄ **Total Time: 10 minutes plus chilling**

BASE

8 creamy nougat-filled
  chocolate bars (each
  1.8 oz/52 g)
1 cup salted butter
8 cups crispy rice cereal

CHOCOLATE TOPPING

2 cups semisweet chocolate
  chips
½ cup salted butter
½ tsp vanilla extract

1. Butter a 13- × 9-inch pan.

2. For the base: In a large pot (about 5 quarts) over medium-low heat, heat the chocolate bars and butter, stirring until melted, smooth, and creamy, with no lumps.

3. Remove from the heat and gently stir in the cereal until completely coated.

4. Press the base mixture firmly into the bottom of the prepared pan (but don't push so hard that you crush the cereal).

5. For the topping: Place the chocolate chips and butter in a large microwave-safe glass measuring cup. Microwave on high power in 20-second increments, stirring after each, until the chocolate chips have almost completely melted (a few lumps are okay). Stir until fully melted, combined, and smooth.

6. Pour the topping over the base, smoothing it over to cover entirely. Refrigerate until the topping is set, about 20 minutes, then slice into 24 squares.

7. Store in an airtight container in layers, with parchment or waxed paper between each layer, at room temperature for up to 5 days or in the freezer for up to 3 months.

CANDY CANE BLONDIES

It's a well-known fact that I will add mint to just about any baked good, dessert, or cocktail I feel will benefit from it, and blondies are no exception. These ooey-gooey, buttery blondies are an excellent basic recipe on their own, but with the addition of mint extract and chopped candy canes, they become the perfect Christmas treat to leave out for Santa!

Makes 2 dozen bars ❄ **Prep Time: 10 minutes** ❄ **Total Time: 40 minutes**

2¼ cups flour

1½ tsp baking powder

1 tsp salt

¾ cup butter

1½ cups firmly packed brown sugar

3 eggs

1 tsp vanilla extract

1 tsp mint extract

¾ cup finely chopped peppermint-flavored candy canes

½ cup chopped white chocolate chips

1. Preheat the oven to 350°F. Butter a 13- × 9-inch baking pan.

2. In a medium bowl, whisk together the flour, baking powder, and salt. Set aside.

3. In a stand mixer with the paddle attachment or in a large bowl using a handheld mixer, beat the butter and brown sugar on medium speed until creamy and light in color. Add the eggs, one at a time, beating well after each. Mix in the vanilla and mint extract until combined. With the mixer on low speed, gradually add the flour mixture, mixing until fully incorporated. Using a wooden spoon, stir in the candy canes and chocolate chips until evenly distributed.

4. Pour the batter into the prepared pan and, with buttered hands, pat into an even layer.

5. Bake for to 25 to 30 minutes or until golden brown on top and a tester inserted in the center comes out nearly clean. (You want to slightly underbake these or they will dry out; they are easily over-baked.) Let cool completely in the pan, then slice into 24 bars.

6. Store in an airtight container in layers, with parchment or waxed paper between each layer, in the fridge for up to 5 days or in the freezer for up to 3 months.

TIP: You can easily play with this basic blondie recipe to create new variations. For example, omit the mint extract and add another teaspoon of vanilla, then replace the candy canes with Christmas-colored sprinkles, white or semisweet chocolate chips, or chopped candied fruit.

Battle of the Puffed Wheat Squares

When it comes to this Canadian Prairie classic, it's the ultimate battle of the sisters. My puffed wheat square recipe (also in book number two, *The Prairie Table*) is practically no-fail, thanks to the marshmallows preventing the mixture from candying, which can yield rock-hard squares. It's chewy and chocolatey, and has the classic taste we all grew up with.

But I popped over to my sister Karami's house one day when she had made her version. I took a bite and immediately picked up something different from my own: instant coffee. It gives the squares such a deep, dark flavor boost that I immediately demanded her recipe. (I'm the older sister, so I get to be bossy like that.) While not quite the traditional Prairie taste, these are simply spectacular, flavor-wise.

So here are our recipes, and you can choose the winner for your family. Just don't tell me if it's my sister's, I don't want to know.

Makes 20 squares ❊ Prep Time: 10 minutes ❊ Total Time: 10 minutes plus setting

KARAMI'S PUFFED WHEAT SQUARES

1 cup packed brown sugar

½ cup light corn syrup

⅓ cup salted butter

2 Tbsp unsweetened cocoa powder

1 tsp vanilla extract

½ tsp instant coffee granules

8 cups puffed wheat cereal

1. Butter a 13- × 9-inch pan.

2. In a medium saucepan, combine the brown sugar, corn syrup, butter, cocoa, vanilla, and coffee. Bring to a boil over medium-high heat, stirring occasionally. Stop stirring and boil for 30 seconds.

3. Place the cereal in a very large bowl. Pour in the sugar mixture and stir until the cereal is coated.

4. Press the cereal mixture firmly into the prepared pan. Let stand for 30 minutes at room temperature, then slice into 20 squares.

5. Store in an airtight container at room temperature for up to 5 days. Do not refrigerate. These will go rock hard after freezing, so it's best just to eat the whole panful within the 5 days and skip the freezer.

see over for my version

KARLYNN'S PUFFED WHEAT SQUARES

½ cup salted butter

½ cup light corn syrup

½ cup granulated sugar

¼ cup packed brown sugar

6 Tbsp unsweetened cocoa powder

1–2 cups mini marshmallows (1 cup = chewy, 2 cups = even chewier)

1 tsp vanilla extract

10 cups puffed wheat cereal

1. Butter a 13- × 9-inch pan.

2. In a medium saucepan, combine the butter, corn syrup, granulated sugar, brown sugar, and cocoa. Bring to a boil over medium-high heat, stirring occasionally. Stop stirring and boil for 1 minute.

3. Remove from the heat and stir in the marshmallows all at once, followed by the vanilla, stirring until the marshmallows are melted in completely.

4. Place the cereal in a very large bowl. Pour in the marshmallow mixture and stir until the cereal is coated.

5. Press the cereal mixture firmly into the prepared pan. Let stand for 30 minutes at room temperature, then slice into 20 squares.

6. Store in an airtight container at room temperature for up to 5 days. Do not refrigerate. These will go rock hard after freezing, so it's best just to eat the whole panful within the 5 days and skip the freezer.

which is your favorite?

MILLIONAIRE'S SHORTBREAD

This is one of THE Christmas dainties on the Prairie: the shortbread crust, caramel filling, and chocolate topping hit all the right notes! Some sea salt is the perfect touch to finish it off.

Makes 30 bars ⁂ Prep Time: 20 minutes ⁂ Total Time: 50 minutes plus cooling

CRUST

2 cups flour

1 cup salted butter, softened

½ cup icing sugar

FILLING

1 cup sweetened condensed milk

1 cup packed brown sugar

½ cup salted butter

3 Tbsp corn syrup

½ tsp vanilla extract

TOPPING

2 cups semisweet or dark chocolate chips

⅓ cup whipping cream or heavy cream

Sea salt flakes, for sprinkling (optional)

1. Preheat the oven to 350°F. Line a 13- × 9-inch pan with parchment paper, leaving enough overhang at either end to use as handles.

2. For the crust: In a medium bowl, using a pastry blender or by crisscrossing two knives, mix together all the crust ingredients until the butter is incorporated and the mixture resembles coarse crumbs.

3. Press the crust mixture firmly into the bottom of the prepared pan.

4. Bake for 15 minutes or until lightly browned. Let cool while preparing the filling.

5. For the filling: In a medium, heavy-bottomed saucepan, combine the milk, brown sugar, butter, and corn syrup. Bring to a boil over medium heat, stirring constantly. Boil, stirring, for 10 minutes or until the mixture is a deep golden-caramel color.

6. Remove from the heat and stir in the vanilla.

7. Pour the filling over the crust. Cool until just warm, then refrigerate until completely cooled and set, about 15 minutes.

8. For the topping: Meanwhile, place the chocolate chips and whipping cream in a small saucepan. Heat over medium heat, stirring, until the chocolate is melted and the mixture is smooth. Let cool for 5 minutes.

9. Spread the topping evenly over the cooled filling. Let cool completely, then slice into 30 bars. Sprinkle with sea salt (if using).

10. Store in an airtight container in layers, with parchment or waxed paper between each layer, in the fridge for up to 5 days or in the freezer for up to 3 months.

Mint Chocolate Brownies

The base brownies of this recipe are great as is, but when you add a mint buttercream layer and top with a chocolate ganache, they become a mint lover's dream come true! If you really want to amp up the mint flavor, add the optional mint extract to the chocolate topping.

Makes 25 squares ❄ **Prep Time: 30 minutes** ❄ **Total Time: 1 hour, 10 minutes plus cooling**

BASE

¾ cup butter

1½ cups granulated sugar

¾ cup unsweetened cocoa powder

3 eggs

1 tsp vanilla extract

¾ cup flour

FILLING

½ cup salted butter, softened

3 cups icing sugar

1 Tbsp whipping cream or heavy cream

1 tsp mint extract

Green food coloring

TOPPING

1 cup semisweet chocolate chips

¼ cup whipping cream or heavy cream

¼ cup salted butter

¼ tsp mint extract (optional)

1. Preheat the oven to 350°F. Line a 9-inch square pan with parchment paper.

2. For the base: In a medium saucepan over medium-high heat, melt the butter.

3. Remove from the heat and stir in the granulated sugar until combined. Stir in the cocoa until combined. Beat in the eggs and vanilla. Add the flour and mix until just combined.

4. Pour the batter into the prepared pan.

5. Bake for 30 to 40 minutes or until the edges start to pull away slightly from the sides. Let cool completely in the pan.

6. For the filling: In a stand mixer with the paddle attachment or in a large bowl using a handheld mixer, beat the butter and icing sugar on medium speed until smooth and creamy. Beat in the cream, mint extract, and enough food coloring to reach your desired color.

7. Spread the filling over the base. Refrigerate while you prepare the topping.

8. For the topping: In a small saucepan over medium heat, combine all the topping ingredients. Stir until the chocolate is melted and the mixture is smooth. Let cool for 5 minutes.

9. Evenly spread the topping over the filling. Let cool until just warm, then refrigerate for 15 minutes or until the chocolate sets. Slice into 25 squares.

10. Store in an airtight container in layers, with parchment or waxed paper between each layer, in the fridge for up to 5 days or in the freezer for up to 3 months.

CHAPTER SIX

CAKES, DESSERT SALADS & PUDDINGS

W hile we all love the treats we eat throughout the season, the desserts that grace the dinner table, whether alongside or right after a Christmas feast, also deserve a chapter! Of course, with my notorious sweet tooth, the only salads I make are dessert salads. But my Ambrosia Salad on page 235 is the original with sour cream—no whipped topping to be found! Trust me, once you try its perfect balance of sweet and sour, you'll never go back to the overly sweet version. Not that I don't love overly sweet desserts . . . see the Pistachio Fluff (page 239) and the Seafoam Salad (page 232).

Every Prairies family, including mine, has a version of the Spiced Carrot Christmas Pudding (page 240). It's the one dessert we have after every single Christmas dinner, without fail. My Grandma Marion used to make it, and now the pudding torch has been passed on to me.

And yes, I had to include fruitcake. You know how it goes with fruitcake: either you love it or you hate it. I come from a long line of fruitcake lovers and just so happened to marry one too, so I included both my mom's mastered light version on page 216 (the secret to its deliciousness is apricot brandy) and a whisky-based, deep-flavored dark version (page 219) that is one of the only recipes I have from my godmother, Auntie Darlene. Make these a solid eight weeks before Christmas and season them weekly with your chosen alcohol— soaking makes all the difference to the taste and texture.

While traditional cakes (i.e., not fruitcakes) don't immediately come to mind when you think of Christmas desserts, there are some that fit the bill. Almost everyone makes a yule log; we just happen to make a mint version, colored green for a Christmas palette (page 227). It's all about the holiday hues, so since the Red Velvet Bundt Cake (page 215) is, well, red, it's also perfect for this time of year. I hope you'll find the perfect recipe to round out your Christmas dinner!

Cranberry Coffee Cake

This is an excellent coffee or teatime cake for the holiday season—or year-round. It has become my new favorite coffee cake, one I've started making on a regular basis. The tang of the fresh cranberries in the cake topped with a sweet cranberry sauce is coffee cake nirvana. Using my Homemade Cranberry Sauce (page 248) rather than canned makes it outstanding.

Serves 12 ❄ **Prep Time: 20 minutes** ❄ **Total Time: 1 hour**

CAKE

3 cups flour

1 cup granulated sugar

3 tsp baking powder

1½ tsp salt

½ cup butter, cold

2 eggs

1 cup milk

1 tsp vanilla extract

1 cup coarsely chopped cranberries

TOPPING

1 cup Homemade Cranberry Sauce (page 248)

¼ cup flour

¼ cup packed brown sugar

¼ cup butter, melted

Pinch of salt

BAKING TIP:
As with all coffee cakes, do not over-bake this, or it will dry out.

1. Preheat the oven to 350°F. Butter and flour a 10-inch spring-form pan.

2. For the cake: In a large bowl, whisk together the flour, granulated sugar, baking powder, and salt. Using a pastry blender or by crisscrossing two knives, cut in the butter until the mixture is fine and crumbly, with the butter the size of peas.

3. In a medium bowl, beat the eggs well, then mix in the milk and vanilla until combined. Add to the flour mixture, mixing until just combined. Fold in the cranberries.

4. Spoon the batter into the prepared pan. Tap the pan gently on the counter a few times to release any air bubbles.

5. For the topping: Place the cranberry sauce in a zip-top bag with a bottom corner snipped off. Using the end of a spoon, create crisscross grooves in the top of the batter, about 1½ inches apart. Pipe the cranberry sauce into the grooves.

6. In a small bowl, combine the remaining topping ingredients, using a fork to claw and toss the mixture until crumbly. Sprinkle over the batter in an even layer.

7. Bake for 35 to 40 minutes or until a tester inserted in the center comes out clean. Let cool in the pan for 30 minutes, then remove the sides of the pan.

8. Store wrapped in plastic wrap at room temperature for up to 5 days, or wrap tightly in plastic wrap, then foil, and freeze for up to 3 months.

CHRISTMAS RED VELVET BUNDT CAKE

Red velvet cake is not something I ever ate growing up, as it's not a traditional dessert here on the Prairies. However, it's been my daughter's number one choice whenever she comes across it in cupcake form. So I would be remiss to not share the recipe I've perfected over the years. (And with it being a festively red cake, and her birthday being just after Christmas . . . and, okay, it might just be my favorite cake now too . . . I had to include it!) I love tang, so I use both sour cream AND buttermilk in my version, along with cornstarch—my secret for a velvety crumb without having to invest in an entire bag of cake flour.

Serves 10–12 ❄ Prep Time: 25 minutes ❄ Total Time: 1 hour, 15 minutes

2¼ cups flour

¼ cup cornstarch

¼ cup unsweetened cocoa powder

1 tsp baking soda

½ tsp salt

½ cup butter, softened

1¾ cups granulated sugar

½ cup vegetable oil

3 eggs

1 cup buttermilk

½ cup sour cream

2 tsp vanilla extract

1½ Tbsp red food coloring

Cream Cheese Frosting (page 249)

Sprinkles

1. Preheat the oven to 350°F. Butter and flour a 10-inch Bundt pan.

2. In a large bowl, whisk together the flour, cornstarch, cocoa, baking soda, and salt. Set aside.

3. In a stand mixer with the paddle attachment or in a large bowl using a handheld mixer, beat the butter and sugar on medium speed until light and fluffy. Beat in the oil until combined. Add the eggs, one at a time, beating well after each. Mix in the buttermilk, sour cream, vanilla, and food coloring until fully combined. With the mixer on low speed, gradually add the flour mixture, mixing until just blended. Do not overbeat!

4. Pour the batter into the prepared pan. Tap the pan gently on the counter a few times to release any air bubbles.

5. Bake for 45 to 50 minutes or until a tester inserted near the inner edge comes out clean, as this can be the last place the cake finishes baking. Let cool in the pan on a wire rack for 30 minutes, then invert the cake onto a wire rack to cool completely.

6. Store in an airtight container at room temperature for up to 3 days, or wrap tightly with multiple layers of plastic wrap and freeze for up to 3 months.

7. Before serving, frost the cake with the cream cheese frosting and garnish with sprinkles. (A frosted cake can also be stored, but it must be refrigerated; it will keep for up to 5 days.)

Light Christmas Fruitcake

I come from a family of fruitcake lovers—and then I married one as well. I LOVE a good fruitcake, and this is my Grandma Marion's tried-and-true recipe that we've been making for decades. Every Christmas season when my siblings and I were young, my mom would gift it to friends and family. She would also bring it to the holiday farmers' markets and sell out every single time! The apricot brandy provides fantastic moistness and flavor, but if you prefer, apple juice is a great substitute.

Makes 3 loaves ❄ **Prep Time: 30 minutes** ❄ **Total Time: 2 hours plus aging**

4 cups flour

2 tsp baking powder

2 cups salted butter

2 cups granulated sugar

6 eggs

1 tsp vanilla extract

1 tsp almond extract

½ cup apricot brandy or apple juice

2 lb sultana raisins

1 cup blanched slivered almonds

1 cup chopped walnuts

4 cups candied mixed peels

1 container (16 oz or 450 g) red and green glace cherries, halved

Spiced rum, apple brandy, or apricot brandy, for soaking

1. Preheat the oven to 300°F. Place an 8-inch square pan with 3 inches of hot water in it on the bottom shelf. Line three 9- × 5-inch loaf pans with two layers of parchment paper each.

2. In a medium bowl, whisk together the flour and baking powder. Set aside.

3. In a very large bowl using a handheld mixer, beat the butter and sugar on high speed until smooth and creamy, about 2 minutes. Add the eggs, one at a time, beating well after each. Mix in the vanilla and almond extract until combined. With the mixer on low speed, gradually add half of the flour mixture, then the brandy, then the remaining flour mixture, mixing well after each until fully incorporated. Using a wooden spoon, stir in the raisins, almonds, walnuts, peels, and cherries until evenly distributed.

4. Divide the batter evenly among the prepared pans, packing it firmly.

5. Bake for 90 minutes or until set. Let cool completely in the pans.

6. Soak three large pieces of cheesecloth (each large enough to wrap one loaf) with rum or brandy until damp but not dripping wet. Wrap each cake tightly with a damp piece of cheesecloth, then wrap lightly with waxed paper and transfer to a large zip-top bag. Store in the fridge for up to 8 weeks. Every week, soak the cheesecloth with brandy again, then rewrap. For best results, let it season for at least 2 weeks.

7. Slice and serve when ready, or store wrapped in plastic wrap in the fridge for up to 3 months or in the freezer for up to 1 year.

AUNTIE DARLENE'S DARK WHISKY FRUITCAKE

Like godmother, like goddaughter. This recipe comes from my Auntie Darlene, who wrote down "a wine glass of whisky." I think my wine glass of whisky is close to hers, so 6 ounces should do the trick: half in the cake and half in the wrapping! You can swap the whisky for rum, brandy—whatever floats your boat. Fruitcake is best when made early and seasoned weekly for up to 8 weeks before Christmas.

Makes 3 loaves ❄ **Prep Time: 30 minutes** ❄ **Total Time: 2 hours plus aging**

3¾ cups sifted flour

2 tsp salt

1 tsp ground cinnamon

½ tsp ground allspice

½ tsp ground ginger

¼ tsp ground nutmeg

9 cups Thompson raisins

2½ cups dried currants

½ cup chopped candied pineapple

½ cup candied mixed peels

½ cup sliced red and/or green glace cherries

1½ cups blanched whole almonds (reserve 24 for topping)

½ cup chopped walnuts

½ cup pecan halves

2 cups butter

2¾ cups packed brown sugar

10 eggs

½ cup cooking molasses

½ cup orange juice

3 oz Canadian whisky, plus more for soaking

1. Preheat the oven to 300°F. Place an 8-inch square pan with 3 inches of hot water in it on the bottom shelf. Line three 9- × 5-inch loaf pans with two layers of parchment paper each.

2. In a very large bowl, whisk together the flour, salt, cinnamon, allspice, ginger, and nutmeg. Stir in all the fruits and nuts until evenly distributed.

3. In a stand mixer with the paddle attachment or in a large bowl using a handheld mixer, beat the butter and brown sugar on high speed until smooth and creamy, about 2 minutes. Add the eggs, one at a time, beating well after each. Mix in the molasses, orange juice, and whisky until combined.

4. Add the egg mixture to the flour mixture and stir until well combined.

5. Divide the batter evenly among the prepared pans, packing it firmly. Decorate the top with the reserved almonds.

6. Bake for 90 minutes or until set. Let cool completely in the pans.

7. Soak three large pieces of cheesecloth (each large enough to wrap one loaf) with whisky until damp but not dripping wet. Wrap each cake tightly with a damp piece of cheesecloth, then wrap lightly with waxed paper and transfer to a large zip-top bag. Store in the fridge for up to 8 weeks. Every week, unwrap the fruitcakes and soak the cheesecloth with whisky again, then rewrap. For best results, let it season for at least 2 weeks.

8. Slice and serve when ready, or store wrapped in plastic wrap in the fridge for up to 3 months or in the freezer for up to 1 year.

Lemon Poppy Seed Cake

Poppy seeds are used prolifically in traditional Ukrainian baking, and pairing them with lemon makes for the ultimate cake. Lemon is such a great pop of summery flavor in the middle of winter, and it's affordable and readily found in stores.

Serves 12 ❄ **Prep Time: 15 minutes** ❄ **Total Time: 1 hour, 5 minutes**

3 cups flour

1½ tsp baking soda

¾ tsp salt

1 cup buttermilk

½ cup poppy seeds

3 Tbsp lemon zest

¼ cup lemon juice

¾ cup butter, softened

2 cups granulated sugar

3 eggs

Citrus Icing or Glaze (page 249), made with lemon zest and juice

1. Preheat the oven to 350°F. Butter and flour a 10-inch Bundt pan.

2. In a medium bowl, sift together the flour, baking soda, and salt. Set aside.

3. In a small bowl, mix together the buttermilk, poppy seeds, lemon zest, and lemon juice. Set aside.

4. In a stand mixer with the paddle attachment or in a large bowl using a handheld mixer, beat the butter and sugar on high speed until smooth and creamy, about 2 minutes. Add the eggs, one at a time, beating well after each. Add the flour mixture and mix until combined. Mix in the poppy seed mixture until just blended.

5. Pour the batter into the prepared pan and use a spatula to smooth the top.

6. Bake for 50 minutes or until the top is browned and a tester inserted near the inner edge comes out clean. Let cool in the pan on a wire rack for 15 minutes, then invert the cake onto the rack to cool completely.

7. Store in an airtight container at room temperature for up to 3 days, or wrap tightly with multiple layers of plastic wrap and freeze for up to 3 months.

8. Before serving, glaze the cake with the lemon icing or glaze. (A glazed cake can also be stored, but it must be refrigerated; it will keep for up to 5 days.)

GUMDROP CAKE

Decadent and delicious gumdrop cake! Perfect for your next party or holiday gathering! I use the brand of gumdrops called Fruitlets, made by Nutty Club, which are ideal because of their already miniature size. But if you can't find these, simply chop up standard-sized gumdrops into small pieces.

Serves 12 ❄ **Prep Time: 15 minutes** ❄ **Total Time: 1 hour, 30 minutes**

2½ cups flour

2 Tbsp cornstarch

2 tsp baking powder

½ tsp salt

1 cup butter, softened

1 cup granulated sugar

4 eggs

2 tsp almond extract

1 tsp vanilla extract

1 cup milk

2¼ cups mini gumdrops (or chopped standard-sized gumdrops)

Citrus Icing or Glaze, made with orange zest and juice (page 249)

1. Preheat the oven to 325°F. Spray a 9- or 10-inch Bundt pan with cooking spray.

2. In a medium bowl, whisk together the flour, cornstarch, baking power, and salt. Set aside.

3. In a stand mixer with the paddle attachment or in a large bowl using a handheld mixer, beat the butter and sugar on high speed until smooth and creamy, about 2 minutes. Add the eggs, one at a time, beating well after each. Mix in the almond extract and vanilla. Add the flour mixture alternating with the milk, making three additions of each and mixing until well combined. Stir in the gumdrops until evenly distributed.

4. Spoon the batter into the prepared pan, spreading it out evenly.

5. Bake for 65 to 75 minutes or until a tester inserted near the inner edge comes out clean. Let cool in the pan on a wire rack for 15 minutes, then invert the cake onto the rack to cool completely.

6. Store in an airtight container at room temperature for up to 3 days, or wrap tightly with multiple layers of plastic wrap and freeze for up to 3 months.

7. Before serving, glaze the cake with the citrus icing or glaze. (A glazed cake can also be stored, but it must be refrigerated; it will keep for up to 5 days.)

Holiday Cheesecake

This is a no-fail cheesecake recipe—as long as you put full trust in me and my instructions! I've tweaked my family recipe's baking times and technique to avoid cracking. Choose from either the shortbread crust or a traditional graham cracker one (see variation). I personally love the shortbread crust for a delicious seasonal twist.

Serves 10–12 ❄ Prep Time: 20 minutes ❄ Total Time: 1 hour, 45 minutes plus resting

SHORTBREAD CRUST

1½ cups flour

1 cup granulated sugar

½ cup butter, softened

1 egg, beaten

½ tsp vanilla extract

FILLING

3 packages (each 8 oz/226 g) cream cheese, softened

2 Tbsp cornstarch

¾ cup granulated sugar

4 eggs

1 egg yolk

½ cup whipping cream or heavy cream

½ cup sour cream

4 tsp vanilla extract

Homemade Cranberry Sauce (page 248), for topping

Sugared Cranberries (page 254), for garnish

1. Preheat the oven to 350°F.

2. For the crust: In a medium bowl, whisk together the flour and sugar. Cut in the butter until fully incorporated. Mix in the egg and vanilla until fully incorporated.

3. Press the crust mixture firmly into an ungreased 10-inch spring-form pan. Prick several times with a fork.

4. Bake for 10 to 15 minutes or until lightly browned. Let cool on a wire rack. Raise the oven temperature to 400°F.

5. For the filling: In a stand mixer with the paddle attachment or in a large bowl using a handheld mixer, beat the cream cheese on medium speed until smooth. Beat in the cornstarch. Add the sugar and beat until fully combined. Add the eggs and egg yolk, one at a time, beating well after each. Add the cream, sour cream, and vanilla, and mix on low speed until fully incorporated. Scrape down the sides of the bowl if there's leftover dough and mix for 1 minute on low speed. Gently pour over the crust.

6. Place a 9-inch square pan with 2 cups hot water on the oven's bottom shelf. Place the cheesecake on the middle shelf. Bake for 10 minutes, then reduce the temperature to 275°F and bake for 1 hour without opening the oven (this is where the trust in me comes in!).

7. Turn off the oven and let the cake rest in the oven for 30 minutes. This ensures a perfectly moist top that won't crack. Transfer the pan to a wire rack and let cool completely. Cover with plastic wrap and refrigerate until chilled, at least 2 hours.

8. Remove the ring from the springform pan and slice the cake. Serve topped with cranberry sauce. Store leftovers in a lidded container in the fridge for up to 3 days.

TRADITIONAL GRAHAM CRACKER CRUST

✳ In step 2, combine 2¼ cups graham cracker crumbs and 3 tablespoons granulated sugar, then stir in ½ cup salted butter, melted, until fully incorporated. Continue as directed with step 3.

MINT YULE LOG

This cake has been the holiday go-to for Prairie folks for decades! Also called a zebra cake, it's formed into a log and sliced, and is the cheater version of the more complex bûche de Noël, which involves baking a cake and rolling it jelly roll–style. We like ours with mint flavor and some green coloring, for extra holiday cheer. It can be a hunt, but the now-rare chocolate wafer cookies are still available—and they're the only ones that work for this recipe! I find them at smaller grocery stores around the holiday season, and you can buy them online as well.

Serves 6 ❄ **Prep Time: 30 minutes** ❄ **Total Time: 30 minutes plus chilling**

Stand mixer with the whisk
attachment

2 cups whipping cream or
heavy cream

2 Tbsp icing sugar

1 tsp mint extract

5–6 drops green food coloring

1 package (9 oz/255 g)
chocolate wafer cookies

1. In the stand mixer, beat the cream on high speed until soft peaks form. With the mixer on medium speed, gradually add the icing sugar, mint extract, and enough food coloring to reach your desired color, beating until stiff peaks form.

2. Spread a heaping teaspoon of whipped cream on each wafer cookie. Press cookies together, whipped cream sides touching, to make sandwiches.

3. On a large platter with a lid, spoon a 1-inch-wide line of whipped cream down the center. Arrange the cookie sandwiches in a log shape on the platter, following the line of whipped cream and placing whipped cream between the sandwiches. Top with the remaining whipped cream. Cover the platter tightly and refrigerate overnight or for up to 2 days.

4. To serve, slice diagonally to create striped pieces.

5. Store leftovers, wrapped on the platter, in the fridge for up to 3 days.

Gingerbread

A lot of people forget that gingerbread is an actual cake, not just houses and cookies! But it is, and it goes perfectly with my Microwave Salted Caramel Sauce or with Cream Cheese Frosting (see tip). Make sure to use cooking molasses instead of fancy molasses for deep flavor, so that the cake will work well with a sweet topping.

Serves 16 ❄ Prep Time: 20 minutes ❄ Total Time: 1 hour

2½ cups flour

2 tsp ground cinnamon

1½ tsp ground ginger

1 tsp ground cloves

1½ tsp baking soda

1 tsp baking powder

½ tsp salt

½ cup butter

½ cup granulated sugar

1 egg

¾ cup cooking molasses

1 tsp vanilla extract

1 cup hot water

Microwave Salted Caramel
    Sauce (page 250), for topping

1. Preheat the oven to 350°F. Butter and flour a 9-inch square pan.

2. In a medium bowl, whisk together the flour, cinnamon, ginger, cloves, baking soda, baking powder, and salt. Set aside.

3. In a stand mixer with the paddle attachment or in a large bowl using a handheld mixer, beat the butter and sugar on high speed until smooth and creamy, about 2 minutes. Add the egg, beating until combined. Mix in the molasses and vanilla until combined. With the mixer on low speed, gradually add the flour mixture, mixing until just combined. Gradually pour in the hot water, mixing until thick, like cake batter.

4. Pour the batter into the prepared pan. Tap the pan gently on the counter a few times to release any air bubbles.

5. Bake for 35 to 40 minutes or until a tester inserted in the center comes out clean. (If not serving immediately, let cool completely in the pan, then transfer to an airtight container and store at room temperature for up to 3 days or in the freezer for up to 3 months.)

6. Serve hot from the oven or cold, drizzled with caramel sauce.

TIP: Cream Cheese Frosting (page 249) is a delicious alternative to the caramel sauce. Let the cake cool completely, then frost before slicing. If you're not serving the gingerbread right away, wait to frost it until just before serving.

CRANBERRY STRAWBERRY MOUSSE SALAD

Nothing says Christmas dinner like a gelatin salad on the table. This one, with its cheery red color, is especially excellent for Christmas. The season's greetings of cranberry flavor paired with a tropical burst of pineapple make for a "salad" the whole family will love!

Serves 12 ❄ Prep Time: 20 minutes ❄ Total Time: 20 minutes plus chilling

2 cups Homemade Cranberry Sauce (page 248)

2 packages (each 3 oz/85 g) strawberry-flavored gelatin powder

1 can (19 oz/540 mL) crushed pineapple, with juice

1 tsp lemon juice

1 cup whipping cream or heavy cream

¼ cup granulated sugar

Sugared Cranberries (page 254) or fresh cranberries, for garnish

1. In a small saucepan over medium heat, heat the cranberry sauce until hot but not boiling.

2. Place the gelatin in a large bowl. Pour in the cranberry sauce and stir until the gelatin has dissolved. Stir in the pineapple and lemon juice until fully combined. Let cool until just warm, then cover and refrigerate until the mixture starts to thicken, about 1 hour.

3. In a stand mixer with the whisk attachment or in a large bowl using a handheld mixer, whip the cream on high speed until it starts to thicken. Add the sugar and whip until soft peaks form.

4. Fold the whipped cream into the gelatin mixture until combined; it will be a nice even pink color throughout.

5. Spoon into a 6-cup gelatin mold (or a bowl of similar capacity) and spread out evenly. Cover and refrigerate overnight or for up to 2 days. (Any longer and it starts to fall apart.)

6. To unmold, dip the bottom of the mold in warm water for 5 seconds, then invert onto a serving plate. Garnish with the cranberries. To serve, cut into 12 slices. (If you have made it in a bowl, there's no need to unmold: simply scoop it out to serve!)

7. Store leftovers in a lidded container in the fridge for up to 2 more days. (It might fall apart, but will still be as tasty as ever!)

Seafoam Salad

Lime gelatin, canned pears, and cream cheese make this retro dessert salad a timeless favorite! The first time I made it myself, I had a flashback to eating it at a Tupperware party when I was a kid, probably in the '70s. The minty-green color makes it perfect for a Christmas dinner table.

Serves 12 ❄ **Prep Time: 10 minutes** ❄ **Total Time: 10 minutes plus chilling**

1 can (28 oz/796 mL) pear halves, with juice

1 package (3 oz/85 g) lime-flavored gelatin powder

1 package (8 oz/226 g) cream cheese, softened

2 Tbsp whipping cream or heavy cream

3 cups frozen whipped topping, thawed, plus more for garnish (optional)

Maraschino cherry, for garnish (optional)

1. Pour 1 cup of the juice from the canned pears into a large microwave-safe glass measuring cup. Microwave on high power until boiling, about 90 seconds. Carefully sprinkle in the gelatin and stir until completely dissolved, with no granules remaining.

2. In a large bowl, beat the cream cheese and cream until smooth. Gradually add the gelatin mixture and mix until well blended. Refrigerate until partially thickened, 40 to 50 minutes.

3. Drain off the remaining pear juice and place the pears in a medium bowl. Using a potato masher or fork, mash until smooth.

4. Fold the pears and whipped topping into the gelatin mixture.

5. Spoon into a 6-cup gelatin mold (or a bowl of similar capacity) and spread out evenly. If you have extra gelatin (I often do!), store the rest in a small bowl. Cover and refrigerate for 2 to 3 hours, until set, or for up to 2 days. (Any longer and it starts to fall apart.)

6. To unmold, dip the bottom of the mold in warm water for 5 seconds, then invert onto a serving plate. To serve, cut into 12 slices. (If you have made it in a bowl, there's no need to unmold: simply scoop it out to serve!) Garnish with additional whipped cream and a maraschino cherry, if desired.

7. Store leftovers in a lidded container in the fridge for up to 2 more days.

AMBROSIA SALAD

Ah, the classic ambrosia salad, also known as 5-cup salad. It has been around since the 1800s. While the mid-century recipe calls for a container of whipped topping (which was invented in 1966, so the switch to using it during that time period makes sense), this is the traditional version using sour cream, which is less sweet and, in my humble opinion, much better. Mandarin oranges have long been associated with Christmas and Christmas desserts, so this salad is very popular during the holiday season.

Serves 8 ❄ **Prep Time: 10 minutes** ❄ **Total Time: 10 minutes plus chilling**

1 cup drained canned whole mandarin orange segments

1 cup drained canned pineapple chunks

1 cup mini marshmallows

1 cup sweetened shredded coconut

1 cup sour cream

Maraschino cherries, for garnish (optional)

1. In a medium bowl, stir together all the ingredients until thoroughly combined. Cover and refrigerate for 3 to 4 hours, until chilled, or for up to 2 days. Serve chilled, garnished with maraschino cherries, if desired, and enjoy!

2. Store leftovers in a lidded container in the fridge for up to 2 more days.

Gingerbread Trifle

I love trifles, not only because they are quick to make, but also because if you accidentally mess up a cake to the point that it breaks when removed from the pan, whipping together a trifle is an easy way to make use of it so you don't have to throw it out in a fit of rage (not that that has ever happened to me, mind you—I'm a civilized woman). This recipe makes such an amazing Christmassy gingerbread-based dessert, you might just mess up the cake on purpose. I hope you love it as much as my family does!

Serves 10 ❄ Prep Time: 30 minutes ❄ Total Time: 30 minutes plus chilling

Stand mixer with the whisk
    attachment

2 packages (each 3.4 oz/96 g)
    lemon-flavored instant
    pudding mix

3 cups whipping cream or
    heavy cream

¼ cup granulated sugar

2 tsp vanilla extract

Gingerbread (page 228)

1. Preheat the oven to 350°F.

2. Prepare the lemon pudding according to the package directions.

3. In the stand mixer, whip the cream, sugar, and vanilla on high speed until light and fluffy and the cream forms stiff peaks when you lift the whisk, 4 to 5 minutes.

4. Cut the gingerbread into 1-inch cubes. Set aside 2 cubes to top the trifle. Place one-third of the remaining cubes in a trifle or other large bowl. Spread one-third of the lemon pudding on top, followed by one-third of the whipped cream. Repeat the layers two more times.

5. Crumble the reserved cake cubes into small crumbs and sprinkle over the whipped cream. Cover with plastic wrap and refrigerate for at least 8 hours or up to 24 hours (the longer, the better!). Serve chilled.

6. Store leftovers in the fridge, wrapped with plastic wrap, for up to 2 days.

PISTACHIO FLUFF

Readers of my first two cookbooks were probably panicking that I hadn't yet included a pistachio pudding recipe. Fear not, here it is, my Christmas gift to you: my absolute favorite dessert salad! Watergate, the Green Stuff, Pistachio Fluff—it's all the same, no matter the name. This salad has all my top sweet-treat favorites: pistachio pudding, pineapple, maraschino cherries, and mini marshmallows . . . it's like it was invented just for me! We prefer homemade whipped cream to premade whipped topping, but you can easily sub in 1½ cups to save time.

Serves 10 ❊ Prep Time: 20 minutes ❊ Total Time: 30 minutes plus chilling

PUDDING

1 can (19 oz/540 mL) crushed pineapple, with juice

1 package (3.4 oz/96 g) pistachio-flavored instant pudding mix

1 cup mini marshmallows

½ cup chopped well-drained maraschino cherries

½ cup chopped toasted pecans (see tip, page 59)

HOMEMADE WHIPPED CREAM

¾ cup whipping cream or heavy cream

1 Tbsp granulated sugar

1 tsp vanilla extract

Cherries, for topping (optional)

1. For the pudding: In a large bowl, combine the crushed pineapple and pudding mix, stirring until the pudding mix has dissolved. Stir in the marshmallows, cherries, and pecans.

2. For the whipped cream: In a stand mixer with the whisk attachment or in a medium bowl using a handheld mixer, beat the whipping cream, sugar, and vanilla on high speed until soft peaks form.

3. Stir the whipped cream into the pudding. Cover and refrigerate for at least 4 hours or, ideally, overnight. Serve within 48 hours.

4. To serve, scoop into bowls and top with cherries (if using) or more whipped cream.

Spiced Carrot Christmas Pudding

Every Prairie family has their version of this pudding. After making the base recipe, with grated carrot and potato, the rest is up to your family's taste! The variations come in when choosing the fruit: dried currants are popular (though not in our family), or you can sub in the same amount of your favorite dried or candied fruits. Not many versions use candied pineapple, but it's one of my favorite parts. Of course, you must top it with brandy brown sugar sauce. It's not Christmas in our house without this pudding!

Serves 12 ❄ Prep Time: 20 minutes ❄ Total Time: 3 hours, 50 minutes

1 cup flour

2 tsp ground allspice

¼ tsp salt

½ cup butter

1¼ cups packed brown sugar

¼ cup fancy molasses

1 cup loosely packed coarsely grated carrots

1 cup loosely packed grated potato, divided

1 cup seedless Thompson raisins

1 cup sultana raisins

¼ cup chopped candied pineapple

1 cup green and red glace cherries, quartered

1 tsp baking soda

Vanilla ice cream

Brandy Brown Sugar Sauce (page 252)

1. Butter a 6-cup oven-safe glass bowl or pudding mold.

2. In a medium bowl, whisk together the flour, allspice, and salt.

3. In a large bowl, using a handheld mixer, cream the butter and brown sugar on medium speed until smooth and creamy. Mix in the molasses until fully incorporated. Stir in the carrots and ½ cup of the potato. Stir in the flour mixture until fully incorporated. Stir in the raisins and candied fruits until evenly distributed.

4. Place the remaining ½ cup of potato in a small bowl, add the baking soda, and stir until dissolved. Stir into the batter.

5. Spoon the batter into the buttered bowl, filling to the top and smoothing evenly. Cover the bowl with a round of parchment paper, then cover tightly with foil. Using baking twine, tie the foil down around the edges of the bowl.

6. Place a footed trivet in a large pot and add water until it hits the bottom of the trivet. Place over medium heat. Place the bowl on the trivet, cover the pot, and bring the water to a low simmer. Reduce the heat to low, keeping the water simmering, and steam the pudding for 3 hours or until a skewer inserted in the center comes out clean. (Remove the foil before poking!) Check on the water every hour and add more as needed.

7. Let cool completely before storing in the fridge. This is best when made 4 to 5 days ahead, and wrapped tightly with plastic wrap in the pudding mold. You can also freeze it for up to 3 months.

8. To serve, steam over medium heat until warmed through, about 30 minutes from chilled or 60 minutes from frozen. Serve by scooping a portion out of the mold, topping it with vanilla ice cream and the brandy brown sugar sauce.

CRANBERRY PUDDING

This cranberry pudding is the perfect way to take advantage of cranberry season, which lasts only a few months in the fall and winter. Orange zest and spices are lovely additions to the traditional recipe. The sweetness comes from the butter sugar sauce, so don't skip it, as the pudding is quite tart on its own.

Serves 12 ❄ Prep Time: 20 minutes ❄ Total Time: 1 hour, 50 minutes

PUDDING

1⅓ cups flour

2 Tbsp orange zest

½ tsp salt

¼ tsp ground cinnamon

¼ tsp ground allspice

¼ tsp ground cloves

⅓ cup hot water

1 tsp baking soda

½ cup fancy molasses

¼ cup packed brown sugar

2 cups coarsely chopped cranberries

BUTTER SUGAR SAUCE

1 cup granulated sugar

½ cup salted butter

½ cup whipping cream or heavy cream

½ tsp vanilla extract

Sugared Cranberries (page 254) or fresh cranberries, for garnish

1. Butter a 6-cup pudding mold or oven-safe glass bowl.

2. For the pudding: In a large bowl, whisk together the flour, orange zest, salt, cinnamon, allspice, and cloves.

3. In a large measuring cup, combine the hot water and baking soda. Stir in the molasses and brown sugar until well combined. Pour into the flour mixture and mix until a soft dough forms. Stir in the cranberries until evenly distributed.

4. Spoon into the prepared mold. Cover the mold with a round of parchment paper, then cover tightly with foil. Using baking twine, tie the foil down around the edges of the mold.

5. Place a footed trivet in a large pot and add water until it hits the bottom of the trivet. Place over medium heat. Place the bowl on the trivet, cover the pot, and bring the water to a low simmer. Reduce the heat to low, keeping the water simmering, and steam the pudding for 1½ hours or until a tester inserted in the center comes out clean. (Remove the foil before poking!). Check on the water every 30 minutes and add more as needed. If serving right away, keep warm in the pot while preparing the sauce.

6. For the sauce: In a medium saucepan over medium heat, combine the sugar, butter, and cream. Stir until well blended and creamy, then stir in the vanilla.

7. To serve, invert the pudding onto a serving plate and garnish with cranberries. Drizzle the sauce over top, slice, and serve warm.

8. This is best eaten the day it's made, but can also be made ahead, cooled, wrapped tightly with plastic wrap in the pudding mold, and frozen for up 3 months. Reheat by wrapping in foil and heating in a 300°F oven until warm in the center, about 45 minutes.

Pumpkin Bread Pudding

This is the perfect all-encompassing Christmas treat for pumpkin spice lovers, whether for Christmas morning breakfast, for the night's dessert, or as a way to use up leftover bread and buns from your holiday meals. It will work with any bread you can cut into 1-inch cubes—fresh French bread, leftover brioche buns, and anything in between. For an adult treat, soak the raisins in rum overnight, then drain and use in the recipe!

Serves 12 ❄ Prep Time: 20 minutes ❄ Total Time: 1 hour, 55 minutes plus chilling

11 cups 1-inch bread cubes

3 cups milk

1 can (14 oz or 300 mL) sweetened condensed milk

1 can (19 oz/540 mL) pumpkin pie filling

2–3 tsp pumpkin pie spice

4 eggs

½ cup raisins

½ cup chopped pecans

Brandy Brown Sugar Sauce (page 252)

1. Grease the bottom and sides of a 13- × 9-inch baking dish with 2 tablespoons melted salted butter.

2. Place the bread cubes in the prepared dish, pressing down lightly into an even layer. Set aside.

3. In a large bowl, whisk together the milk, condensed milk, pie filling, and pie spice to taste (see tip). Whisk in the eggs until well combined. Stir in the raisins until evenly distributed.

4. Pour the milk mixture over the bread cubes. Cover tightly with plastic wrap and refrigerate for at least 5 hours or, ideally, overnight.

5. Preheat the oven to 350°F.

6. Sprinkle the pecans over the bread pudding, pressing them gently into the top. Cover with foil.

7. Bake for 30 minutes. Remove the foil and bake for 55 to 65 minutes or until firm in the center and the internal temperature is at least 165°F. Let cool slightly. (If not serving immediately, let cool completely in the dish, then wrap the pan with plastic wrap and store in the fridge for up to 3 days.)

8. Serve warm or cold, drizzled with the brandy brown sugar sauce.

BAKING TIP: When deciding how much pumpkin pie spice to add, remember that you're seasoning a LARGE amount of bread cubes! I usually add the third teaspoon of spice, but I am crazy about it. Be sure to taste before adding the eggs in the next step.

CHAPTER SEVEN

ICINGS, FROSTINGS, SAUCES & GARNISHES

Consider this the mix-and-match chapter! Almost everything here can be paired with numerous treats in this book, even if I haven't stated so explicitly. The combinations are endless, so I'll let you use your imagination about which desserts you want to pour the caramel sauce (page 250) over. (The answer is everything. You want to put that on everything.)

Although you can always opt for a store-bought version of these icings and sauces if you're pressed for time (and I love a good store-bought icing—just check out the Gumdrop Frosting Fudge on page 135), the one I would suggest making yourself is my Homemade Cranberry Sauce (page 248), because stores always get in fresh cranberries during the holidays. The difference in taste and quality is night and day, and it's most apparent when topping my Cranberry Coffee Cake (page 212): the vanilla and cinnamon in my homemade version make the canned varieties pale in comparison.

Royal Icing (page 250) is the ultimate icing for decorating cookies. There's no need to use raw eggs, thanks to the wide availability of meringue powder! Just make sure you buy pasteurized meringue powder (most are). And don't use liquid food coloring. The amount needed to achieve the color you want adds too much liquid, so your icing will never dry. Use icing gels instead (the ones used for coloring buttercream), available in little pots at craft superstores. Red takes a LOT of gel to get it past pink tones (which I usually end up with anyway; you can't win them all!), but there are endless ready-to-buy shades of greens. Warning: while this drier gel is great for icings, it also likes to dry on your surfaces—quickly! I try to clean up any loose bits on the counter, paddle, and bowl right away, rather than scraping the cement-like crust off later.

Enjoy the recipes and have fun mixing and matching!

Homemade Cranberry Sauce

It will come as no surprise that I make cranberry sauce just so I can use it in desserts like my Cranberry Coffee Cake (page 212) or simply drizzle it over vanilla ice cream for a quick treat. That said, you can also serve this cranberry sauce with your roasted bird for the big day!

Makes 4 cups ❄ Prep Time: 5 minutes ❄ Total Time: 35 minutes

1 cup water

1 cup granulated sugar

3½ cups thawed frozen or fresh cranberries

2 Tbsp freshly squeezed orange juice

½ tsp orange zest

¼ tsp ground cinnamon (optional)

⅛ tsp vanilla extract (optional, see tip)

Orange peels or cinnamon sticks, for garnish (optional)

1. In a medium saucepan over medium-high heat, combine the water and sugar, stirring until the sugar has dissolved. Add the cranberries and orange juice, and bring to a boil. Boil, stirring, for 10 to 15 minutes or until the berries start to pop and dissolve into the mixture. Using a wooden spoon, crush them against the side of the pot. Boil, stirring, until the mixture has thickened and reduced into a sauce. Add the orange zest and boil, stirring, for 5 minutes.

2. Remove from the heat and stir in the cinnamon and vanilla (if using), adding more to taste if desired.

3. Store the cooled sauce in an airtight container in the fridge for up to 1 week or in the freezer for up to 3 months. Serve cold.

TIP:
If making this sauce to serve with turkey, I prefer to leave out the vanilla.

Citrus Icing or Glaze

This easy topping tastes wonderful on almost every cake in the book, from Gumdrop Cake (page 223) to Cranberry Coffee Cake (page 212). It's a fantastic base recipe that you can tweak to your liking, making a thicker icing or a thinner glaze, and experimenting with various citrus fruits. Lime also works great!

Makes ½ cup ❄ Prep Time: 5 minutes ❄ Total Time: 5 minutes

1¾ cups icing sugar

1 Tbsp orange or lemon zest

2 Tbsp–¼ cup orange or lemon juice

1 tsp salted butter, melted

1. In a large glass measuring cup, whisk together the sugar, zest, and juice until there are no lumps. Use 2 tablespoons of juice for a thicker icing or ¼ cup juice for a thinner glaze. Add the butter and whisk until smooth.

2. If it's not pourable enough to glaze a cake, you can microwave it for about 30 seconds until it is, then let rest until it cools and thickens slightly.

3. Store in an airtight container in the fridge for up to 3 days. To use, microwave until pourable.

Cream Cheese Frosting

This is the perfect frosting for Christmas, pairing with everything from Gingerbread (page 228) to Christmas Red Velvet Bundt Cake (page 215).

Makes 2 cups ❄ Prep Time: 10 minutes ❄ Total Time: 10 minutes

1 package (8 oz/226 g) cream cheese, softened

½ cup salted butter, softened

2–3 cups icing sugar

1 tsp vanilla extract

1. In a stand mixer with the paddle attachment or in a large bowl using a handheld mixer, beat the cream cheese on medium speed until smooth and light-textured. Add the butter and beat until well combined. Beat in 2 cups of the icing sugar, then taste and add more, ¼ cup at a time, until you have reached the perfect tang and sweetness for your taste! Mix in the vanilla until combined.

2. Store in an airtight container in the fridge for up to 3 days or in the freezer for up to 3 months.

Royal Icing

With meringue powder readily available in stores nowadays, it's never been easier to make royal icing at home without having to use raw egg whites. The key to ensure that this icing dries into a sweet, crackly topping is to use concentrated icing gels to color your icing. Liquid food coloring would thin it out too much.

Makes 1½ cups ❄ Prep Time: 10 minutes ❄ Total Time: 10 minutes plus drying

4 cups sifted icing sugar

3 Tbsp pasteurized meringue powder

½ tsp vanilla, mint, or almond extract

6–10 Tbsp room-temperature water

Concentrated icing gels, for coloring

TIP:
If using sprinkles, decorate the icing while it's still wet.

1. In a stand mixer with the whisk attachment or in a large bowl using a handheld mixer, whip the sugar, meringue powder, vanilla, and 6 tablespoons of the water on high speed until smooth peaks form, about 5 minutes. For thicker icing that holds its shape (for piping shapes onto cookies), don't add any more water. For thinner icing that floods cookies, lift the whisk and see if the icing drizzles down, pools out, and smooths. If it does not, beat in more water, 1 tablespoon at a time, until it does.

2. Divide the icing into small bowls and gradually add one color of gel to each, mixing thoroughly until the desired color is reached.

3. Store in an airtight container at room temperature for up to 1 week. Before using, beat with a mixer until smooth and shiny again.

4. To pipe, spoon into icing bags with the desired tip (or disposable icing bags with the tip cut off) and pipe onto cookies. Set aside and let dry fully, about 2 to 3 hours, depending on humidity.

Microwave Salted Caramel Sauce

This is one of my favorite cheat recipes when I need a quick caramel sauce. Use it on any of the Christmas puddings, on gingerbread, or simply over vanilla ice cream.

Makes 1 cup ❄ Prep Time: 1 minute ❄ Total Time: 3 minutes

1 cup packed brown sugar

½ cup whipping cream or heavy cream

¼ cup melted butter

¼ tsp salt

1. In a large microwave-safe bowl, whisk together all the ingredients. Microwave for 2 minutes or until thickened, checking the consistency halfway through. Stir well. Store in an airtight container in the fridge for up to 1 week.

Brandy Brown Sugar Sauce

This sauce is our traditional topping for the Spiced Carrot Christmas Pudding (page 240) or drizzled over my Pumpkin Bread Pudding (page 244) for an adult breakfast treat! Any leftovers are great heated up and enjoyed on vanilla ice cream. For a family-friendly version, leave out the brandy.

Makes 2 cups ❄ Prep Time: 5 minutes ❄ Total Time: 15 minutes

¾ cup packed brown sugar

½ cup salted butter

1½ cups boiling water

2–3 Tbsp brandy (optional)

1½ Tbsp cornstarch

¼ cup cold water

1. In a medium saucepan over medium heat, melt the brown sugar and butter, and heat until bubbling rapidly.

2. Remove from the heat and stir in the boiling water—watch out, it can spit! Return to medium heat and whisk in the brandy to taste (if using). Bring back to a boil.

3. In a small bowl, combine the cornstarch and cold water. Gradually whisk into the sauce and cook, stirring, until thickened. Serve hot or let cool before storing.

4. Store the cooled sauce in an airtight container in the fridge for up to 3 days. To use, reheat in the microwave, whisking every 20 seconds and adding a bit more water if it's too thick.

Cinnamon Cranberry Simple Syrup

As soon as fresh cranberries hit the store, you'll be making this simple syrup to use with EVERYTHING. In mocktails or cocktails, or over ice cream or a simple vanilla cake, this cold weather–inspired simple syrup is excellent for any and all seasonal delights.

Makes 4 cups ❄ Prep Time: 5 minutes ❄ Total Time: 20 minutes

3 cups fresh cranberries

2 cups granulated sugar

2 cups water

2 cinnamon sticks

1. In a medium saucepan over medium-high heat, combine all the ingredients and bring to a simmer, stirring until the sugar dissolves completely. Simmer until the berries have popped or softened enough to squish when pressed gently with a wooden spoon. Using a potato masher, gently crush to release the juices.

2. Using a fine-mesh strainer or, even better, cheesecloth, strain into a mason jar.

3. Store in the fridge for up to 1 month; discard once it's cloudy.

Candied Ginger & Simple Syrup

With this recipe, not only do you create delicious candied ginger to spice up your Christmas baking, you also get simple syrup to use in cocktails such as the Ginger Gimlet Martini (page 265). While the recipe is a bit finicky and time-consuming, both the ginger and the syrup last quite a long time, so you can get them done early, before diving into the holiday entertaining frenzy.

Makes about 2 cups of each ❄ **Prep Time: 20 minutes** ❄ **Total Time: 30 minutes plus drying**

1 lb fresh gingerroot

5 cups water, divided

1½ cups granulated sugar, divided

1. Peel the ginger and cut into ⅛-inch-thick slices, either circles or long strips.

2. Place the ginger in a medium saucepan with 2 cups of the water. Bring to a boil over medium-high heat and boil for 15 minutes.

3. Drain, then add another 2 cups of water and bring to a boil again. Boil for another 15 minutes or until the ginger is tender. Drain again.

4. Place the remaining 1 cup of water and 1 cup of the sugar in a saucepan. Add the ginger and bring to a low boil over medium heat. Reduce the heat and simmer for 15 minutes or until the mixture thickens into a syrup.

5. Using a slotted spoon, transfer the ginger to a colander, reserving the syrup. Drain the ginger well and set aside.

6. Let the syrup cool, then store in an airtight container in the fridge for up to 1 month or in the freezer for up to 6 months.

7. Place the remaining ½ cup of sugar in a shallow bowl. Add the ginger slices and toss to coat. Shake off any excess sugar and spread the slices on a baking sheet or wire rack and let dry overnight. I use a fan to speed up the process and completely dry them, shaking the pan and turning them over every so often.

8. Store the candied ginger in an airtight container in layers, with parchment or waxed paper between each layer, in the fridge for up to 6 months or in the freezer for up to 1 year.

Sugared Cranberries

These sugared cranberries are best made the day before you want to enjoy them. Use them to garnish dishes and cocktails and as a sweetly sour treat. They only last a couple of days before they start to weep liquid. You can toss them again with sugar to coat, but it's best to enjoy them before that happens.

Makes 2 cups ❄ **Prep Time: 20 minutes** ❄ **Total Time: 25 minutes plus drying**

2 cups granulated sugar (approx.), divided

¼ cup water

1 bag (12 oz/340 g) fresh cranberries

1. Line two large baking sheets with parchment paper.

2. In a medium saucepan over medium-high heat, heat ½ cup of the granulated sugar and the water, stirring until the sugar has dissolved completely. Bring to a low boil, then add the cranberries and stir until coated. Remove from the heat.

3. Using a slotted spoon, remove the cranberries, holding them to drain off as much liquid as possible before spreading them in a single layer on one of the prepared baking sheets. Let dry for 1 hour, shaking the pan once or twice to shift the cranberries around so that all sides get exposed to the air and dry out. They will be tacky to the touch.

4. Place the remaining sugar in a lidded container. Add the cranberries, cover, and shake to coat completely. Spread out on the second prepared baking sheet and let dry overnight. I put a fan on them to make sure they dry out, and shake the pan a few times throughout—it works like a charm!

5. Store in an airtight container at room temperature for up to 2 days. If they start to weep liquid, you can coat them in more sugar.

CHAPTER EIGHT

COCKTAILS & PUNCHES

A nd now it's time for Mr. Kitchen Magpie to take over, closing the book with a final chapter of holiday cocktails and drinks! (It's the only time I'll let him get the last word.)

When it comes to entertaining over the holidays, drinks are among the first things I plan out. Whether it's cocktails like the Christmas Sunrise (page 266) or classically cozy Whisky Mulled Wine (page 269) for the adults, or mocktails for the kids and non-indulgers, it's an important part of the festivities.

And mocktails aren't only for the kids! There are plenty of folks who don't partake in alcohol, so to make sure I've got everyone covered equally, I've included some delicious non-alcoholic options. Both my Retro Sherbet Party Punch (page 263), with its floating sherbet, and my Homemade Eggnog (page 261) are delicious—but if you do want to give the eggnog a little kick, it's easy to add rum.

Over the years, I've become less and less inclined to purchase liqueurs if I can make them myself—and I can, and so can you! Simply start with a vodka base, then add ingredients from there. As you'll find in this chapter, I've got some great recipes that have won the hearts of our relatives and had them asking how to make their own! There's always one person (or more) in the family who is ultra-tough to buy for. (In my case, it's my father-in-law.) So what's better than tucking homemade liqueur under the tree with a recipe card so they can re-up whenever they want? Nothing. Nothing is better. They will love you for it.

Christmas and New Year's are the perfect time to break out the fancy glasses and punch bowls from the back of the cabinets—let them see the light of day one more year! Rinse them off, polish them up, and let's get to making some amazing holiday drinks!

Enjoy!
Mike (Mr. Kitchen Magpie)

STOCKING YOUR CHRISTMAS BAR

Nothing is worse than realizing, come Christmas Eve, that you forgot to stock up for the holidays and now have to rush out to gather those last-minute ingredients for your hot toddies and martinis. So here's what you'll need to stock up your bar to fully embrace the Christmas spirit (pun intended). A huge plus is that you'll likely already have on hand plenty of the pantry and perishable items from baking everything in this book!

BAR TOOLS

* BAR SPOON
* BOSTON SHAKER (TWO-PIECE COCKTAIL SHAKER)
* CHEESECLOTH
* COCKTAIL PICKS OR SKEWERS

* COCKTAIL STRAINER
* ICE BUCKET
* MESH STRAINER
* MOLD FOR LARGE ICE CUBES
* WINE OPENER

GLASSWARE

* CHAMPAGNE FLUTES
* HIGHBALL GLASSES
* HURRICANE GLASSES
* MARTINI GLASSES

* ROLY POLY GLASSES
* SHOT GLASSES
* WHISKY TUMBLERS
* BRANDY GLASSES

LIQUOR CABINET

* ANGOSTURA BITTERS
* BOURBON
* CHAMPAGNE
* CHOCOLATE-FLAVORED VODKA
* CRÈME DE CACAO
* CRÈME DE CASSIS
* CRÈME DE MENTHE

* DRY VERMOUTH
* IRISH WHISKEY
* ORANGE BITTERS
* RED WINE
* SCOTCH
* TRIPLE SEC
* VODKA

PANTRY

- ALMOND EXTRACT
- BROWN SUGAR
- CHOCOLATE SPRINKLES OR SHAVINGS
- CINNAMON STICKS
- GRANULATED SUGAR
- GROUND CINNAMON
- GROUND NUTMEG
- INSTANT COFFEE
- LIQUID HONEY
- STAR ANISE PODS
- SWEETENED CONDENSED MILK
- VANILLA EXTRACT
- WHOLE CLOVES

PERISHABLES

- CHOCOLATE SYRUP
- EGGS
- GINGERROOT
- HALF-AND-HALF (10%) CREAM
- LEMONS
- LIMES
- MARASCHINO CHERRIES
- ORANGES
- ORANGE JUICE (FRESH FOR SMALLER QUANTITIES)
- PINEAPPLE JUICE
- RAINBOW SHERBET
- WHIPPING CREAM OR HEAVY CREAM
- WHOLE CRANBERRIES (FRESH OR FROZEN)
- WHOLE MILK

SODA

- GINGER ALE
- LEMON LIME SODA

Clockwise from top left: Homemade Eggnog (see opposite), Homemade Irish Cream (page 262),

White Chocolate Russian (page 262), Season's Greetings Grasshopper (page 263)

Homemade Eggnog

No Christmas is complete without eggnog, and this recipe has been tested and approved by the whole family! Why run out to the store, only to stress about whether you'll be able to find enough eggnog for everybody, when you can easily make your own at home? This recipe is great, because you can simply add some rum for the adults, while the kids and those who abstain can enjoy the eggnog as is.

Makes 9 cups ❄ **Prep Time: 10 minutes** ❄ **Total Time: 20 minutes plus chilling**

7 cups milk, divided

1 cup granulated sugar

1 tsp ground cinnamon

5 whole cloves

2 tsp vanilla extract, divided

12 egg yolks (see tip)

¼ tsp ground nutmeg, or to taste

1. In a large saucepan over medium heat, combine 4 cups of the milk with the sugar, cinnamon, cloves, and ½ teaspoon of the vanilla. Bring to a simmer, stirring constantly, then remove from the heat.

2. In a large bowl, beat the egg yolks until fluffy. Temper the eggs by gradually whisking in 1 cup of the milk mixture until the eggs are warm. Gradually pour the tempered eggs into the milk mixture in the saucepan, whisking constantly until combined completely.

3. Return the saucepan to medium-high heat and cook until the mixture thickens and reaches 165°F on an instant-read thermometer. Do not let it boil!

4. Pour the egg mixture through a mesh strainer into a pitcher or other container. Cover with plastic wrap and refrigerate for 2 hours.

5. Add the remaining 3 cups milk, the remaining vanilla 1½ teaspoons, and nutmeg, whisking well.

6. Store in a covered pitcher or container in the fridge for up to 5 days.

TIP: You can use the leftover egg whites to make the Chocolate Meringue Corn Cereal Cookies on page 97 or Meringue Christmas Tree Pops on page 140.

Homemade Irish Cream

Just like my Homemade Amaretto (page 271), this Irish cream makes a great Christmas gift for that impossible-to-buy-for person in your life. In fact, whip up a batch of both, finish each with a bow, and you've got the perfect gift!

Makes 4 cups ❄ Prep Time: 5 minutes ❄ Total Time: 5 minutes

1 cup Irish whiskey

½ cup whipping cream or heavy cream

½ cup milk

1 can (14 oz or 300 mL) sweetened condensed milk

2 Tbsp chocolate syrup

1 tsp instant coffee granules

1 tsp vanilla extract

1. Place all the ingredients in a blender and blend on low for 20 to 30 seconds or until smooth and creamy.

2. Store in an airtight container in the fridge for up to 2 months. A drink pitcher with a sealing lid, like the glass one shown in the photo on page 260, works perfectly for this at home. For gifting, pour into clean glass bottles with lids. Shake well before serving.

White Chocolate Russian

It's time to update the classic white Russian with my modern twist of chocolate vodka, homemade Irish cream, and whipped cream! Chocolate vodka really makes this drink shine, and Smirnoff makes a great one!

Makes 1 cocktail ❄ Prep Time: 5 minutes ❄ Total Time: 5 minutes

Ice cubes

1 oz chocolate-flavored vodka

1 oz Homemade Irish Cream (page 262)

2 oz half-and-half (10%) cream

Whipped cream, for garnish

Chocolate sprinkles, for garnish

Maraschino cherry, for garnish (optional)

1. To a Boston shaker filled with ice, add the vodka, Irish cream, and cream. Shake until the shaker is cold to the touch.

2. Pour through a cocktail strainer into a chilled martini glass (see tip, page 266).

3. Garnish with whipped cream, chocolate sprinkles, and a cherry (if using).

Season's Greetings Grasshopper

The grasshopper cocktail is dessert in a glass. In fact, few desserts taste this darn good: the chocolate and mint flavors are so strong and decadent, it's like drinking one of Karlynn's Mint Chocolate Brownies (page 208). I mean, you could skip making the brownies and just whip up this cocktail, but my actual advice is to make both.

Makes 1 cocktail ❄ Prep Time: 5 minutes ❄ Total Time: 5 minutes

Ice cubes

¾ oz crème de menthe

¾ oz white crème de cacao

¼ oz whipping cream or heavy cream

Chocolate shavings, for garnish

1. To a Boston shaker filled with ice, add the crème de menthe, crème de cacao, and cream. Shake until the shaker is cold to the touch.

2. Pour through a cocktail strainer into a coupe or similar small cocktail glass.

3. Sprinkle with chocolate shavings.

Retro Sherbet Party Punch

This is a quick and easy party punch, perfect to serve at Christmas to keep the kids busy while the adults enjoy some cocktails (read on!) by the fire. If you make sure all your ingredients are already chilled, you can simply combine them and serve, instead of keeping a large punch bowl in your fridge.

Makes 1 punch bowl (20 servings) ❄ Prep Time: 10 minutes ❄ Total Time: 10 minutes

2 quarts rainbow sherbet

4 cups ginger ale, chilled

4 cups lemon lime soda, chilled

4 cups pineapple juice, chilled

1 jar (13.5 oz/375 mL) maraschino cherries, drained

1 lemon, sliced

1 lime, sliced

Ice cubes (optional)

1. Scoop the sherbet into a punch bowl and add the ginger ale, lemon lime soda, and pineapple juice. Stir slowly, ensuring you don't decarbonate the drink.

2. Stir in the cherries until evenly distributed. Float the lemon and lime slices on top.

3. To serve, pour into punch cups with ice (if using).

Clockwise from top left: Christmas Party Kir Royale (see opposite), Ginger Gimlet Martini (see opposite);

Christmas Sunrise (page 266), Perfect Christmas Crantini (page 266)

Christmas Party Kir Royale

Kir royales are synonymous with Christmas get-togethers. Maybe it's the red color or the champagne that makes them so festive. This aperitif combines crème de cassis, made from freshly pressed black currants, with champagne to create a delicious bubbly cocktail for pre–Christmas dinner sipping. The amount of crème de cassis can be adjusted to taste; we prefer a stronger champagne taste in our kir royales.

Makes 1 cocktail ❄ Prep Time: 3 minutes ❄ Total Time: 3 minutes

⅓ oz crème de cassis, or to taste

5 oz champagne, chilled

Lemon twist, for garnish

1. Pour the crème de cassis into a champagne flute and top with the champagne.

2. Garnish with a lemon twist.

TIP: This cocktail is popular for parties, as you can make many drinks at once using one bottle of champagne. A 750 mL bottle has 25 ounces, so get out five champagne flutes, put ⅓ ounce crème de cassis in each, then divide the champagne among them. Garnish with lemon twists and voilà, drinks for your guests in mere minutes!

Ginger Gimlet Martini

Karlynn loves a good martini. In fact, it's the most requested kind of drink in our house—other than wine, that is. This ginger martini is easy, tastes great, and really soothes on a cold winter day. It's also a wonderful way to feature our homemade ginger simple syrup and candied ginger.

Makes 1 cocktail ❄ Prep Time: 5 minutes ❄ Total Time: 5 minutes

Ice cubes

2½ oz vodka

¾ oz Ginger Simple Syrup (page 253)

½ tsp freshly squeezed lime juice

Lemon or lime twist, for garnish

Candied Ginger (page 253) on a cocktail pick, for garnish

1. To a Boston shaker filled with ice, add the vodka, simple syrup, and lime juice. Shake until the shaker is cold to the touch.

2. Pour through a cocktail strainer into a chilled martini glass (see page 266).

3. Garnish with a lemon or lime twist and a cocktail pick of candied ginger.

Christmas Sunrise

The sunrise cocktail is a classic, having been around for quite some time. While it's traditionally made with grenadine, orange juice, and vodka, my variation uses a cranberry simple syrup to give it more of a holiday spin.

Makes 1 cocktail ❄ Prep Time: 3 minutes ❄ Total Time: 3 minutes

1 oz Cinnamon Cranberry
    Simple Syrup (page 252)

1 oz vodka (optional)

¾–1 cup orange juice

Orange slice, for garnish
    (optional)

Sugared Cranberries (page 254)
    on a cocktail pick, for garnish
    (optional)

1. Pour the simple syrup and vodka (if using) into a hurricane glass. Pour the orange juice over top to create a layered effect—do not stir.

2. If desired, garnish with an orange slice and/or a cocktail pick of sugared cranberries.

Perfect Christmas Crantini

The crantini (or cranberry martini) is a delicious festive drink that's sure to get your guests smiling at your next holiday bash. It makes great use of the Sugared Cranberries as a garnish!

Makes 2 cocktails ❄ Prep Time: 5 minutes ❄ Total Time: 5 minutes

Ice cubes

1 oz vodka

½ oz triple sec

½ oz dry vermouth

2 oz cranberry juice

Sugared Cranberries (page 254)
    on cocktail picks, for garnish

1. To a Boston shaker filled with ice, add the vodka, triple sec, vermouth, and cranberry juice. Shake thoroughly until the shaker is cold to the touch.

2. Pour through a cocktail strainer into two chilled martini glasses (see tip).

3. Garnish each with a cocktail pick of sugared cranberries.

TIP: Chill your martini glasses in the freezer for 20 minutes before you shake the drink. You will have perfectly frosty glasses that keep your martini cold!

Clockwise from top left: Cranberry Bourbon Sour (see opposite), Whisky Mulled Wine (see opposite), Retro Sherbet Party Punch (page 263)

Cranberry Bourbon Sour

As soon as the first snowflakes fall, leave your summertime sangrias behind and turning to seasonally inspired drinks. There is almost nothing better than a basic bourbon sour, but one with cranberry simple syrup along with the traditional citrus juices? Winner! You have the perfect cocktail for your winter soirees. Like the Christmas Party Kir Royale (page 265), this is a great recipe to scale up or down.

Makes 4 cocktails ❄ Prep Time: 5 minutes ❄ Total Time: 5 minutes

Large ice cubes

1 cup bourbon, chilled

½ cup freshly squeezed lemon juice, chilled

½ cup orange juice, chilled

½ cup Cinnamon Cranberry Simple Syrup (page 252), chilled

Fresh cranberries (or Sugared Cranberries, page 254) on a cocktail pick, for garnish

1. Fill four whisky tumblers or brandy glasses with ice cubes.

2. In a large pitcher, combine all the ingredients, stirring well. Pour over the ice in each glass.

3. Garnish each with a cocktail pick of cranberries.

TIP: Chilling all the ingredients beforehand eliminates the need to shake them over ice. Yes, I keep my bourbon in the fridge. Doesn't everyone? Please don't answer that.

Whisky Mulled Wine

Mulled wine is a traditional winter drink ideal for snowy Christmas nights. Make sure to serve this warm. I find it works best with Canadian Club whisky, a brand sweeter than most; more traditional recipes use brandy. Feel free to modify the spices, for your own unique spin—though Karlynn and I have found this combination to have the best balance of flavors.

Makes 4½ cups ❄ Prep Time: 5 minutes ❄ Total Time: 2 hours, 5 minutes

1 bottle (750 mL) red wine (Cabernet Sauvignon or similar)

⅔ cup Canadian whisky

8 whole cloves

4 cinnamon sticks

4 whole star anise pods

4 pieces Candied Ginger (page 253)

1 orange, sliced

1 lemon slice

1. Place all the ingredients in a slow cooker. Cover and cook on low for 2 hours. Strain and serve warm.

Clockwise from top left: Homemade Amaretto (see opposite), Amaretto Manhattan (see opposite),

Kris Kringle's Godfather (page 272), Holiday Hot Toddy (page 272)

Homemade Amaretto

My homemade amaretto came about when I was trying to come up with a good present for Karlynn's father one Christmas. He's notoriously difficult to buy for, and since he has always been a big fan of amaretto, I decided to brew him a bottle and then supply him with everything he needs to make his own at home whenever he wants. It's a very simple recipe that produces some of the best amaretto I've personally had, not to mention it's a great, inexpensive way to keep stocked up on the stuff without having to hit the liquor store when you run out—which, considering how good this is, might be often!

Makes 1 bottle (about 750 mL) ❄ **Prep Time: 5 minutes** ❄ **Total Time: 15 minutes plus chilling**

1 cup granulated sugar

½ cup packed brown sugar

1 cup water

2 cups vodka

2 Tbsp almond extract

2 tsp vanilla extract

1. In a medium pot over medium heat, bring the granulated sugar, brown sugar, and water to a boil, stirring until the sugar is completely dissolved.

2. Remove from the heat and stir in the vodka, almond extract, and vanilla. Let cool completely.

3. Using a funnel, pour the amaretto into an airtight bottle and refrigerate for at least 2 hours or, ideally, overnight.

4. Store the sealed bottle at room temperature in a dark place (like a cupboard) for up to 6 months.

Amaretto Manhattan

This cocktail is derived from one I had at a martini bar on a Mexican cruise I took with Karlynn. I made a few adjustments to suit my tastes, and this is the result. I tend to especially enjoy hard-liquor cocktails, like Manhattans and martinis, during winter and over the holidays, and this is one of my personal favorites.

Makes 1 cocktail ❄ **Prep Time: 5 minutes** ❄ **Total Time: 5 minutes**

Ice cubes

2 oz bourbon

½ oz Homemade Amaretto (see above)

½ oz dry vermouth

2 dashes orange bitters

Maraschino cherry on a cocktail pick, for garnish

1. Chill a martini glass in the freezer for 10 minutes. To a Boston shaker filled with ice, add the bourbon, amaretto, vermouth, and bitters. Shake until the shaker is cold to the touch.

2. Pour in the cocktail through a cocktail strainer into the chilled martini glass.

3. Garnish with a cherry on a cocktail pick.

Kris Kringle's Godfather

Next to a good old-fashioned, this is my favorite drink. Switch up the classic recipe by using my home-made amaretto and some good Scotch. What's nice about this drink is that you can drastically alter the flavor by changing the type of Scotch. Looking for something a bit smoky? Simply use a peated Scotch instead of a blended one, and it's a whole different drink!

Makes 1 cocktail ❄ Prep Time: 5 minutes ❄ Total Time: 5 minutes

Large ice cube

2 oz Homemade Amaretto (page 271)

1 oz Scotch

2 dashes Angostura bitters

1. Place the ice cube in a whisky tumbler. Pour in the amaretto and Scotch. Add the bitters and stir with a bar spoon.

TIP: This is a great gift for the Scotch lover. Make my Homemade Amaretto (page 271), pair it with a nice Scotch, buy the bitters, and then wrap them all up together, with this recipe written out.

Holiday Hot Toddy

Nothing beats a hot toddy on a cold day. I have memories of my father making this in a pot over a small propane stove on ice fishing trips to keep warm while waiting for the fish to bite. While I haven't drunk a hot toddy in that setting yet myself, it's on my bucket list now that I've perfected the recipe! The classic cinnamon-spiced drink warms you from the inside out, but my addition of nutmeg and cloves brings back memories of Christmas in a heartbeat.

Makes 1 cocktail ❄ Prep Time: 5 minutes ❄ Total Time: 10 minutes

1 cup boiling water

2 oz Scotch

2–3 Tbsp liquid honey

3 whole cloves

Pinch of ground nutmeg

1 cinnamon stick

½ oz freshly squeezed lemon juice

2 lemon slices, divided

1. In your mug of choice, combine the boiling water, Scotch, honey to taste, and cloves. Sprinkle with the nutmeg, then add the cinnamon stick, lemon juice, and 1 slice of lemon.

2. Let stand for 3 to 5 minutes to meld the flavors and cool the drink enough to enjoy.

3. Garnish with the remaining lemon slice.

Cranberry Bourbon Sour (page 269)

THANK-YOUS

Writing a cookbook during a pandemic has been quite the experience. When I was putting this book together throughout 2020 and 2021, I seemingly had all the time in the world, being stuck at home, but with two kids doing school at home for over a year, we all know it wasn't quite the stretches of downtime we might've first thought it would be. And here we are, with book number three! With that said, of course, there are so many people who have helped me along the way.

A big thank you to Appetite by Random House and Robert McCullough for letting me move the publishing date back a year. While I like to think I am superwoman, there was no way I could have completed the manuscript by the date we first chose AND guided my son through his last year of high school (at home!) AND made sure he graduated AND helped my daughter navigate her first year of high school courses online AND run my business—all during a global pandemic. And I was right. But here I am now, with BOTH children graduated and this book completely done and published!

Thank you to my editor, Whitney Millar, who had the tough job of taking my website style of writing and helping me craft it into cookbook style—they are so very different! Thank you, Sue Sumeraj, for your excellent editing help. Another thanks goes to Judy Phillips, who was the perfect proofreader for this book. And a big thank you to Kate Sinclair for the book design.

As always, thank you to my readers who bought my first and second cookbooks, giving me the street cred to write this Christmas one that I have always wanted to write. There are more and more of you every year, growing our online family bigger all the time.

Thank you to my sister, Karami: my number one recipe tester, even though she hates making candy. I literally could not have completed the book without her help. Also, a big thank you to my nephew Deklen, who came over numerous times to clean my studio kitchen after I baked all day—that's no small feat!

Thank you to my recipe taste-testers: my mom, Donna; my dad, Wilf; and my neighbors, Claudia and Bryce, who tasted-tested at least half the book.

Thank you to Dallas Curow of Luminarie Creative for the amazing family photos in this cookbook. It's always a joy for me to be on the OTHER side of the camera for once!

As always, thank you to my friends who kept in touch over Zoom and texts; you helped me survive the loneliness!

Kade and Ivy, I am so very proud of you for everything you had to sacrifice and overcome the past couple of years. We Gen-Xers thought we were tough, but your generation has had to be even tougher, more compassionate, and more understanding. Thanks for doing your part during the pandemic, for taste-testing, for cleaning, for not eating frozen desserts when I told you I needed them for photos. You two are the best kids anyone could ask for. Love you.

And last but not least, to the man behind the cocktail magic, the shaker of martinis, the cleaner of dishes, and the husband of the decade, Mike, aka Mr. Kitchen Magpie. Thank you for taking care of everything—and I mean everything—while I wrote this book.

INDEX